Victory Through Surrender

E. STANLEY JONES

Victory Through Surrender

ABINGDON PRESS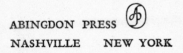

NASHVILLE   NEW YORK

VICTORY THROUGH SURRENDER

ISBN 0-687-43748-2

Library of Congress Catalog Card Number: 66-21189

PRINTED AND BOUND AT NASHVILLE,
TENNESSEE, UNITED STATES OF AMERICA

Contents

Introduction

The question: "What happens to the self in the Christian faith?" the original title of this book, was raised acutely in one of our Christian Ashrams by the director of the Ashram. He was an able businessman, publisher of medical books, and had recently come into a transforming spiritual experience. In the "Morning of the Open Heart," when the group shared their quests in answer to the questions: "Why have you come? What do you want? What do you need?" this director said: "I used to think my self was something to be cultivated, now I wonder if it isn't a cancer to be cut out." He oscillated in his thinking between cultivation and a cancer—the self as something to be cultivated and the self as a cancer to be cut out.

Unwittingly he put his finger upon two schools of thought and attitude toward the self—the school of self-realization and the school of self-renunciation. But

7

strangely enough both these schools of thought and attitude miss the Christian attitude toward the self. This "miss" is important, for if you take the wrong attitude toward your self it is vital, for your self is not a subject of discussion but a point of decision, not an academic school of thought but "a school of hard knocks where the school colors are black and blue."

The difference between the emphasis on self-realization or on self-surrender seems to be this: in self-realization you try to realize your self, for all the answers are in you. In self-surrender you surrender your self to Jesus Christ, for all the answers are in Him. One leaves you centered on you—a self-centered and self-preoccupied person, albeit a religious person. The other loses his self and finds it. For self-realization only comes through self-surrender. You realize your self when you realize Him, and you realize your self when you surrender to Him. That is the heart of this book.

What you think about your self will determine what your self will be. And what your self is now will determine whether you live in heaven or hell now, for your self *is* your heaven or hell now.

To have a wrong idea about the self may produce a wrong self and a wrong self may mean a misspent life. In a small mission plane I went over the spot in Zambia, Africa, where Hammarskjöld met his tragic death. The pilot of the mission plane, who lived in Zambia, told me that they found in the wreckage of the U.N. plane the open map of Nadolo, a town in a section near Leopoldville, Congo, instead of the map of the city of Nadola,

Zambia, the destination of the plane. The map of the Nadolo section showed that the pilot had a thousand feet more than he actually did have in landing at Nadola, for Nadola is higher than Nadolo. So he crashed in an open field in the night, thinking he had a thousand feet more than he actually had. He had the wrong map. The difference of an "o" and an "a" was the difference between death and life—and a very precious life.

If you have the wrong mental map of your self, you will probably come to wrong landings, a disaster instead of a destination.

But this book is not an academic description of the right mental map of your self. Rather it is a book out of life. I have had an opportunity—no credit to me—as perhaps no other man has ever had to look intimately into the lives of people in East and West and see how those selves are working. This opportunity has come, first of all, through our Round Table Conferences, held in India and other parts of the East, for a greater part of my fifty-eight years of missionary work. We gather in each city and town, where possible, the leading men of all faiths and of no faith and say to them something like this: Here we are a group of people using religion as a working hypothesis of life. What have you verified through that hypothesis, that working way to live? We have had the dogmatic, the controversial, the comparative, and the traditional attitudes and approaches toward religion. Let us take an approach more akin to the method of science. In the scientific approach there are three steps: experimentation, verification, and sharing of verifications. We have been experimenting with this matter of religion, using it as a working hypothesis of life. What have we verified? What have we found in experience? I suggest that no one argue, nor preach at the rest of us, nor discuss abstractly our faith, but tell what it has brought to us in experience.

For years I have listened sympathetically. I have not summed up conclusions at the close, but have simply added my own personal word and let it all stand for what it is worth. A Hindu commented: "I have never been in this kind of meeting before—it is a kind of Judgment Day on our lives." It has been—on our lives and not merely on our conceptions of life.

Then again, for twenty-five years we have had in East and West in our Christian Ashrams what we call "The Morning of the Open Heart." It is perhaps the distinctive thing in that movement, for we start not with an attempt to find verbal answers to verbal questions, but we start with a quest. The first step in that quest is a diagnosis. "What do I need?" I began this—of all places—in a garden party in India, the place of chit-chat and gossip. If I had had time to think I would never have tried it, but on the spur of the moment I gathered a group to one side and asked them: "What do you need?" And they responded—amazingly. And they have done so, everywhere around the world with no exceptions. This takes place in groups of from forty to four hundred. The size of the group makes no difference. I tell my needs first of all. I tell them, "I'm only a Christian-in-the-making." They respond, taking hours at it, for if there is an instinct in the human heart to conceal there is also a deeper instinct to reveal.

How is the response? Varied of course, but always one thing comes to the surface—always: the struggle with the self. The self is the meeting place, the center, of problems and possibilities. All else is marginal.

This is what they say: "I came to real transformation six months ago. I saw myself and didn't like what I saw." "I came to find myself. My people think I'm dedicated. I am—I'm dedicated to myself." "I was a mountain of self-righteousness and disdain, now all melted." "I used to be a house devil—I thought all the problems were in others. My blood pressure was 260. Now it's normal. My home is different, happy, so am I." "I need to surrender myself. I live in fear of the work I am to do." "In seminary they told me I had a deep anxiety. One who doesn't have the Holy Spirit is continually trying to prove to others that he is a Christian." "I am so full of needs. My greatest need is to surrender myself—lose myself in Christ. I take a handful of pills. I seem to be running away from something." "I fight back, feel afraid of dominant people. I have had forty-eight hospitalizations." "I've been self-centered and unforgiving." "How can I overcome self-centered ways?" "I need self-forgetfulness." "I want to surrender, but I'm afraid, so I'm full of doubts." "Been wrestling with myself. My greatest need is to admit I have a need." A pastor: "I'm a 'self-holic'— I'm addicted to myself." A Swedish woman: "I came here with a self I don't like, and yet I have to live with myself."

A man put it this way: "Everywhere I go 'I' spoil everything." A skeptic said: "I'm glad I don't believe in eternal life. I wouldn't want to live with myself forever."

Of one man it was said: "He is a walking civil war." Talking to a youth group I said: "That girl was a civil war." At the close another girl came up to me and said: "Well, if that girl is a civil war, I'm a world war." Then she told me how she became a world war: "I heard all this talk that you have a right to taste all experience, including sex experience, apart from morality and apart from God and I went out and pursued it, and I've been a world war ever since." Thus it goes.

The self is the one and only thing we own. It is the one thing we brought into the world and it is the one and only thing we will take out of the world, and the one thing we have to live with intimately day by day, hour by hour, minute by minute. So the kind of self you are determines your life happiness or your life hell. Someone has said: "The most used word in hell is 'I.' "

To be centered in your self is to be in hell—now.

A pastor's wife pulled me into a vestry and blurted out thus: "All my life I've lived to charm people to myself. Now everybody has found me out and I've lost my influence with everybody. Even my little boy of five has found me out and I've lost my influence with him." She was distracted. She had made herself god and her god had let her down. The self was never intended to be the center of the universe.

This devastating effect of making the self god reaches

12

from a pastor's wife to the great of the world. William Barclay tells of the tragic story of Oscar Wilde.

One of the tragedies of the nineteenth century was the career of Oscar Wilde. He had a brilliant mind, and won the highest academic honours; he was a scintillating writer, and won the highest rewards in literature; he had all the charm in the world, and he was a man whose instinct it was to be kind; yet he fell to the temptation of unnatural vice, and came to prison and disgrace. When he was suffering for his fall he wrote his book *De Profundis* and in it he said: "The gods have given me almost everything. But I let myself be lured into long spells of senseless and sensual ease. . . . Tired of being on the heights I deliberately went to the depths in search for new sensation. What the paradox was to me in the sphere of thought, perversity became to me in the sphere of passion. I grew careless of the lives of others. I took pleasure where it pleased me, and passed on. I forgot that every little action of the common day makes or unmakes character, and that therefore what one has done in the secret chamber, one has some day to cry aloud from the house-top. I ceased to be lord over myself. I was no longer the captain of my soul, and did not know it. I allowed pleasure to dominate me. I ended in horrible disgrace." *

Whether it be in the parsonage as with the pastor's wife, or on the stage of the world as with Oscar Wilde, when self becomes the center, becomes God, devastation reigns—and there are no exceptions.

Someone asked the head of a mental institution: "I

* The *Letters to the Galatians and Ephesians* (Philadelphia: The Westminster Press, 1958), pp. 116-17.

suppose these people in here are beside themselves?" "Oh no," he replied, "they are very much themselves. They don't think of a thing except themselves. They are pickled in themselves. That's why they are here."

A mother and father described their daughter to me: "Everything is o.k. as long as everything goes her way, but the moment anything crosses her will she explodes." The girl was in and out of mental institutions and was very religious. But whether in the institution or in a home or in a religious gathering, the result was the same —explosions and devastation, for the self was at the center.

I have given my life to reconciliation—reconciliation between man and God, man and his brother, and man and himself. This endeavor has been worldwide among all races and tribes and peoples. The problem is the same everywhere—the self, the self-centered self, the self-preoccupied self, the unsurrendered self.

A woman said to me: "I've found you out, you have only one remedy—self-surrender." I laughed and said: "I'm glad you have found me out, for I've found myself out. I cannot go down any road on anything with anybody who has problems without running straight into the necessity of self-surrender. All else is marginal, this is central. I have only one remedy, for I find only one disease—self at the center, self trying to be God.

I have just come from Indonesia where a gentle and lovable people are being whipped up into a war frenzy by Sukarno: "Crush Malaysia." What is the sin of Malaysia? The reply: "They have neo-colonialism operative in Malaysia." The answer is: "Suppose they have, what is that to Indonesia?" Incidentally, I don't believe they have neo-colonialism in Malaysia, for colonialism is in the process of liquidating itself; it is on its way out everywhere with one or two spots trying to hold its own. But suppose neo-colonialism is there, why upset the peace of that island world because a neighbor has something in it that you don't like?

The symptoms of self-centered frustration are the same, whether in Sally and Sam in a home or in Sukarno on his island throne, ruling over a hundred million people—the symptoms are the same and they are these: "I am what I am because you are what you are. If you were different I would be different. It is all your fault." The self-centered blame their problems on others. The self at the center is off-center and hence the recurring problems, individual and collective.

This is the center of the diseases of humanity—the self out of place. All else in symptom—this is the disease. Quacks treat symptoms, doctors treat diseases.

Will the Christian faith turn out to be a quack, treating the symptoms of individual and world diseases? Or will it turn out to be a physician—the great physician, putting His finger on the spot, the sore spot of the world's problems? And will that touch be healing?

We now turn to answer those questions. If there is no clear-cut workable answer we stumble from crisis to crisis. If there is an answer we go from cure to cure.

E. STANLEY JONES

1

The Non-Christian Answers

Before we go to the Christian answer we must pause to look at the non-Christian answers and ask what happens to the self under their systems.

Many ancient systems have come to the question of what is to be done with the self and have come to many differing answers. The answers coming out of the East have been, in large measure, answers that show world-weariness. The world is *maya*, illusion, a sport thrown out from God as a magician throws out an unreal world of illusion. It is God's *lila* or sport, a play. Nothing real in it. The "knowing" see this and treat the world as such. They stand inwardly apart from the *samsara* and its illusions.

This view of the world is in head-on collision with modern trends in East and West, for those trends ask for and demand change in this world of ours—agriculture must be improved, social conditions must be changed or abolished, man as man must be given new opportunity, new equality open to all, exploitation of man by man must be ended, the earth has a future and that future is in our hands to change. In this changed intellectual and social climate *maya* itself seems *maya*. It just doesn't fit. Shankarachariya, the great Indian philosopher, wrote fifteen volumes on *maya*. Modern India, bent on a new India, socially, industrially, and intellectually, dismisses it with a sentence—*maya* is *maya*.

That world-weariness goes deeper in Eastern thought —the world-weariness turns to personality-weariness. The personality, the self, is the focal point of all our problems. As long as the self is there the problems are there. So Buddha focused this pervasive disillusionment about the self into the decisive sentence: "Existence and suffering are one." As long as you are in existence you are in suffering. Then the only way to get out of suffering is to get out of desire. For it is desire that makes the wheel of existence, of rebirth, turn round. So cut the root of desire, become desireless even for life. Then you will go out into that passionless, actionless state called Nirvana, literally the state of "the snuffed-out candle." "Is there any existence in Nirvana?" I asked a Buddhist monk. "How can there be?" he replied. "There is no suffering in Nirvana, hence no existence." Buddha would get rid of the problems of the self by getting rid of the self.

That is the most devastating answer ever given to the problem of the self—get rid of the self. All the philosophical attempts to save the self under Buddhism end in sacrificing Buddhism itself. Buddhism stands stark

18

clear: the self is to be got rid of if the problems of life are to be solved. This is spiritual *hari-kari*.

When we turn to Vedantic philosophy we find a milder answer, but radical still. The Vedantic philosophy says that Brahma is the only reality. But Brahma is the Impersonal. So the devotee sits and in meditation affirms: "Aham Brahma"—I am Brahma. He tries to pass from the personal self to the Impersonal Essence, Brahma. When that transition is made the personal self is absorbed into the Impersonal Essence and the problems of the self are over. Just as a raindrop loses itself in the ocean and is absorbed, so the individual self is lost in the ocean of Impersonal Essence. The solution is the dissolution of the individual, personal self.

That is the answer of the Vedantic philosophy which has been described as "the philosophy of a few, the religion of none." For religion means relationship. But Brahma in its highest state is the "Nirguna," without relationships. You cannot say your prayers to the law of gravitation, nor commune with a multiplication table. There must be the answer of the Personal to the personal, if there is to be religion.

Then there is the answer of the Bhakti schools—the devotion of the personal to the personal gods or God. But even the Bhakti schools are tinged with world-weariness and personality-weariness. I visited a Hindu widows' home where the inmates chanted in unison for six hours a day the name of Sita-Ram—Rama, one of the gods, and Sita, his wife. But this devotion was so absorbed in Sita-Ram that their faces were a blank—the blankest faces I've ever seen anywhere. To all intents and purposes the separate selves had been absorbed in the object of their devotion. It was a gradual attrition of the self.

A Bhakti devotee visited our Ashram at Sat Tal, India. I asked him his name and he replied: "Ram, Ram." I asked him where he had come from and he replied, "Ram, Ram." Where was he going? "Ram, Ram." What did he want? "Ram, Ram." I could get no other reply, for he had vowed to use no name except "Ram, Ram." This was high devotion, but very expensive to the self—it was gone. His face was expressionless. Rama was everything—he was nothing.

As a result of all this self-losing effort, what happens? Is the self eradicated? No, religion is compartmentalized among the people, put into sacred days, sacred festivals, sacred forms and ceremonies, but secularism takes over the basic drives and the basic attitudes. Burma builds its golden temples to Buddha, bows before him and his self-elimination and then turns and becomes the most world-loving and life-loving people of the world. India is the most religious people of the world, pays its tribute of folded hands to the philosphies and temple worship and then goes out to live life on a secular basis. The self put out at the door of self-eliminating philosophies comes back through the window as secularism. The self eliminated here comes back there. The sadhus, or holy men, who have renounced most are called "the sky-clothed"—they are naked. In the great Magh Mela tens of thousands of these sadhus were gathered together in Allahabad to bathe at the confluence of the Ganges and the Jumna rivers at a specially propitious time. Each group of sadhus was assigned its hour of procession and bathing. A quarrel arose over the order of precedence, a riot took place, and hundreds of pilgrims were trampled to death in the ensuing mad rush. They were sky-clothed, but their feet were on the earth and demanded precedence. The self came back clothed with its self and naked in its demands to be first.

A Brahmin youth riding his bicycle was confronted with a broken chain. He had no other means to tie it together again except his Brahmin sacred cord which he wore under his garments. Without hesitation he used the cord to tie together the broken chain. When he finished the repair he said to himself and to his companions: "There, that sacred cord has at last done me some good." Unless the sacred gears into the secular and transforms it, it is being quietly laid aside as irrelevant. The self eliminated in religion returns as the self contaminated in secularism.

When we turn from this world-weariness and personality-weariness on the part of the philosophies and religions of the East to modern psychology we find a complete reversal of the attitudes toward the self. Modern psychology has three affirmations about the self: know thy self; accept thy self; express thy self. Just as I am compelled to reject the Eastern view of the self, so I am also compelled to reject this modern psychological view of the self. What is the matter with these three basic

21

attitudes of modern psychology toward the self? And why, if applied, do they result in such meager results? Marginal benefits? Yes. Central and fundamental benefits? Questionable, or no.

Why? What is basically wrong with these three affirmations about the self? Take the first: know thy self. But how can you really know your self by studying your self in relation to your self, and other human selves, in a purely material environment? It is all earth-bound, lacks any eternal meaning or goal. Animals may be satisfied with this world, but man cannot be satisfied this side of God, his Creator and Redeemer. You can only know yourself in relation with your Heavenly Father. You are a child of God and are in the process of being made in the likeness of the Son of God—in the likeness of the most beautiful and the most influential character ever seen on this or any other planet. Then and then only do you know your self. All other knowing, however knowledgeable it may be, is marginal knowing and can only affect the margins of the self. So the best that secular psychology can do is to improve the self, here and there. Cure it from its basic disease? No. For it leaves untouched its basic relationship with God. And with that untouched the basic disease of self-centeredness remains —remains unhealed.

I sent my book, *Conversion*, to Dr. Boss, the head of the international psychoanalytic association of Europe. I thought he would toss it in a corner, unread. Instead he wrote: "This is the kind of a book we need, a book on conversion. Those psychiatrists, who are not superficial,

22

have come to the conclusion that the vast neurotic misery of the world could be termed a neurosis of emptiness. Men cut themselves off from the root of their being, from God, and then life turns meaningless, goalless, empty—and sick. Then we get them as psychiatrists."

Then listen to the head of the American Psychiatric Association, Dr. Kenneth A. Appel: "After a person has been psychoanalyzed he has to have something to take the place of the anxiety of nothingness which remains. He needs something to give him a faith in God."

Or, if you can't listen to psychiatrists, then listen to H. G. Wells: "Religion is the first thing and the last thing and until a man has found God he begins at no beginning and works to no end. He may have his friendships, his partial loyalties, his sense of honor. But all these things fall into place, and life falls into place only with God—only with God." Note that last phrase: "life falls into place only with God—only with God." But secular psychiatry does not begin with God or end with God, and hence it cannot help "life" to "fall into place." It stands helpless before the final demand—something to help life to fall into place. So the self doesn't know its self because it doesn't know God.

Second: accept thy self. But how can you accept an unacceptable self, a self full of conflicts and contradictions, full of guilt and frustrations, inferiorities and inhibitions, full of its self? To ask a man to accept himself —that kind of a self—is to ask the impossible. If he does accept that kind of a self on that level, then he himself

23

is unacceptable to himself. A man wrote to a club resigning: "I can no longer belong to a club that will accept a man like me as a member." After all a man has his standards, whatever he may be, and to ask him to accept himself as he is brings revolt. Only when he has been changed, or is being changed, into another and different man can he accept himself. So when secular psychology asks a man to accept himself as he is it is rejecting God, the moral law and the man's conscience and the psychiatrist's conscience—if he has any left after giving that advice continuously.

Third: secular psychology says: Express thy self. But if you have a dozen people together all of whom have been taught to express themselves—what have you got? I asked that in a group in America, and a Baptist pastor replied: "You've got a Baptist Church!" He might have said: "Methodist Church, Episcopalian Church, or anyone of them." You have the stage set for clash and confusion and jealousy and strife.

The advice of modern psychology points toward self-assertion, means to put your self in the center. And anything that leaves you at the center is off-center. It feeds the disease it is trying to cure, namely, self-centeredness.

What is wrong with these three affirmations of modern psychology? What do they lack? They lack the thing which the Christian faith offers, namely, self-surrender. Note I didn't say, "demands" self-surrender, but it *offers* self-surrender. For self-surrender is more of an offer than a demand. It is a demand also—a demand of human nature, for human nature cannot find itself except it find it in a will and purpose beyond itself. From our side it is a demand, from God's side it is an offer.

But whether an offer or a demand, the deepest necessity of human nature is to surrender itself to something, or someone, beyond itself. Your self in your own hands is a problem and a pain; your self in the hands of God is a possibility and a power.

The Non-Christian Answer
and goal a will and purpose toward itself. For we find in experience that God is love and is our ... But whether an effort at adjustment, the verbal ... bit of exhortation: it is merely ... of ... ... binding itself, ... in ... ... a ... and a ... ... self to the ... of God

2

The Christian Answer

If the non-Christian answers, both religious and psychiatric, are inadequate, what has the Christian faith to offer? If it fails here, it fails. For the self is the center of life, individual and collective, and if the self is unhealed, unadjusted, out of place, then life as a whole is unhealed, unadjusted, out of place.

The Christian answer must not be a verbal answer—a kind of sprinkling rose water on a cancer to make it more acceptable. It must heal it. Its answer must not be verbal but vital. I was in an Express office in Paris, jammed with people in the summertime; the air was fetid, for the windows were closed. An attendant went around spraying the air with perfume—spraying the foul air instead of throwing open the windows to let in fresh air. If we attempt to spray this subject of the self with perfumed words the end will be frustration, for the unredeemed and unhealed self will rise up to mock us.

As I understand it the Christian faith in its New-Testament form asks nothing less and nothing more than self-surrender to God. I say nothing more, for the Self-realization cults always spell the self with a capital S, meaning you are to realize your self as God. This quest to identify your self as the divine Self ends in a quest. It never arrives. I have searched India from the Himalayas to Cape Cormorin for over half a century to find a person who has arrived at the realization of the self become the Self, become God. I have never found one. It is an illusion. The self is created, a creature, and can never become the Creator. "Thou hast made him a little less than God," says the Psalmist. That "little less" important. Man is "made in the image of God," but was never intended to become God. And the attempt to become God is the central sin of religion. It is an attempt to enthrone the self as God, which is the height of self-assertion. And the height of sin. This proud claim to be God is the sin that made Lucifer descend from the heights to the depths.

A swami who had the reputation of having realized that his self was the divine Self was asked by a friend of mine: "Are you divine?" And he replied, "No, I'm a sinner." I listened to a lecture by a Westerner who had adopted this philosophy that you must realize your self as the divine Self. In the midst of his address he toppled the lamp chimney on the table. He swore. The self was a very human self. A toppled lamp chimney toppled his claims. "There is nothing covered."

If the Christian faith does not teach that the self is to

27

become God, neither does it teach self-mortification. "True, it has an air of wisdom, with its forced piety, its self-mortification, and its severity to the body; but it is of no use at all in combating sensuality" (Col. 2:23 NEB). Self-mortification is self-defeating, for it focuses the attention on the self—to watch it, to mortify it, to keep it under. It is a law of the mind that "whatever gets your attention gets you." If your self gets your attention, even a fighting attention, it will get you. You will be a self-preoccupied person, and a self-preoccupied person is a self-defeated person. I have watched it on a wide scale in India—self-mortification ends in a mortified self. The sadhus of India, the holy men, dedicated to self-mortification, have become a national problem, so much so that the government has taken the problem in hand and has set up Sadhu Rehabilitation Centers, centers where sadhus are turned from useless self-mortification and beggary into useful citizens contributing to the welfare and uplift of the country. I have been invited to speak before one of these Sadhu Rehabilitation Centers. For those who are dedicated to self-mortification contribute nothing to themselves and nothing to the country. It is self-defeating and nation-defeating.

If the Christian faith sails between the Scylla of self-deification on the one hand and the Charybdis of self-mortification on the other, what is its path? Its path is self-surrender. Note I do not say self-commitment. You may be committed to a person or a project and not surrendered to that person or project. You may be committed to another in marriage by marriage vows, but not inwardly surrendered to the other person. A soldier may be committed to military service because he has to be by government orders, but he may not be inwardly surrendered to it—he is there under inner protest. Self-surrender is the strongest and most comprehensive word I know, and it needs just such a strong word to meet what is involved.

For what is involved is this: We are to hand back to God the self that is handed to us by the Creator; to surrender the one and only thing we own. A hard demand? It seems so. But I cannot soften it for the New Testament doesn't soften it. Jesus puts it thus: "And to all he said, 'If anyone wishes to be a follower of mine, he must leave self behind'" (Luke 9:23 NEB). And the greatest follower of the centuries, Paul, interprets that as meaning in his case: "I have been crucified with Christ" (Gal. 2:19 NEB). Then he puts it as a broad, comprehensive appeal: "Therefore, my brothers, I implore you by God's mercy to offer your very selves to him: a living sacrifice" (Rom. 12:1 NEB). The Authorized Version says: "Your bodies," but this version says: "Your very selves."

This demand then seems to be absolute and it demands the ultimate—the you, your self. Not merely your time, your loyalty, your trust, your service, your money, but it demands you—the self—in self-surrender. No wonder a Finnish newspaper reporter, after her group had finished getting details and views in general, paused to ask a question which was bothering her: "Why is God so cruel, why does He demand so much of us?" Meaning,

why does God demand the one and only thing I own—
the me, my self, my one ewe lamb? It seemed to her that
she would be consenting to her extinction. Another
woman, a bundle of misery, replied to me when I suggested that she surrender herself to God: "Why if I did
that I would be at God's mercy." She felt that to surrender to God meant that God would take advantage of
that surrender and have an opportunity to make her miserable, when she by her own self-will had made herself
a bundle of misery!

No wonder people are surprised when you present self-
surrender as the basic Christian demand. It is often not
emphasized as the basic Christian demand. A theological
student attended one of our Ashrams and said: "Your
emphasis here on self-surrender amazes me. I've gone
through my whole theological course and I've never
heard the term self-surrender." What was the theological
course? A set of beliefs to be believed, or a moralism to
be followed, both of them leaving the esential self untouched. A book on pastoral counseling says in the pref-
ace: "Let no one think that in the reading of this book
he will be converted." When I finished the book I remarked to myself: "No danger of anyone being converted, for he never uses the word, or presents the idea, of
self-surrender. He deals with the marginal ideas of fears,
worries, anxieties, resentments, but never once of self-
surrender. These fears, worries, anxieties, resentments are
all rooted in the unsurrendered self.

Just as my fingers are rooted in the palm of my hand, so
all these outer sins are rooted in the unsurrendered self.

Why do we get angry and "blow our top"? Because someone has crossed the self. Why do we lie? Because we
think it will be some advantage to the self. Why are we
dishonest? Same reason. Why are we impure? Because
we think it will be some pleasure to the self. Why are we
jealous and envious? Because someone is getting ahead
of the self. All these outer sins are only fruit—the unsurrendered self is the root; the outer sins are symptoms, the
unsurrendered self is the disease. Quacks treat symptoms,
doctors treat diseases. Religion that treats outer symptoms and leaves untouched the central disease, the unsurrendered self, is religious quackery.

The word "radical" refers to "the root." The Christian
faith is radical, for it goes to the root of all our problems,
individual and collective, and deals with the unsurrendered self by self-surrender. It is therefore the one
true physician of the soul. All else is tinkering.

What happens when we surrender to God? Is the soul
wiped out, canceled for all intents and purposes? Is self-
surrender the kind of surgery to the soul that lobotomy
surgery is to the mind when the nerve is cut and the
patient is relieved of his anxieties, but at high price—he
becomes more or less a vegetable? What really happens
in self-surrender to God?

Some seem to imply, or directly teach, that the self is
wiped out. A beautiful hymn in our hymnbooks varies
the end of each stanza. First, "All of self and none of
Thee"; second: "Some of self and some of Thee";
Third: "None of self and all of Thee." It seems that the
self is gone—"none of self"—God is all. Another lovely

31

hymn says: "Perish self in Thy pure fire," the self perishes. Some Christian sects deliberately try to cancel and crush out the self. A Christian sect in Japan is called the "No-self Sect." As a proof that the self is gone the devotees stand under a waterfall in the dead of winter and let the icy waters flow over them. That is to be proof that the self is gone. But the spectacle is usually carried out in the presence of an admiring crowd, a sign that the self has come back! The passage in I Cor. 13:3 in the margin reads: "I may dole out all I possess, or even seek glory by self-sacrifice." The self-sacrifice may be a refined species of self-assertion and self-glorification. The self is still there.

By no known process or method can the self be eliminated. It is a part of us, a very important part—it is us! Put the self out of the door, it will come back by the window, usually dressed up in religious garments, but the same self still.

Peter said to Jesus: "We have left all to follow Thee, what do we get?" They had left all, all except themselves. The "what do we get?" gives away the case. The self is still there.

What happens to the self when surrendered to God? Does He wipe it out, or wipe it clean? He wipes it clean of selfishness. The very act of self-surrender gives Him the opportunity to cleanse us from selfishness with our consent and cooperation. Having cleansed us from our central selfishness He gives the self back to itself. When we obey the deepest law of the universe it works: "whoever would save his life will lose it"—center yourself on your self and the self will disintegrate. Every self-centered person is a disintegrating person. Center yourself on your self and you won't like yourself—and no one else will like you. But the rest of that verse is just as true: "whoever loses his life for my sake he will save it"—lose yourself in the will of God by self-surrender and you will find your self again. It is a paradox, but you are never so much your own than when you are most His. Bound to Him you walk the earth free. Low at His feet you stand straight before everything else. You suddenly realize that you have aligned yourself with the creative forces of the universe so you are free—free to create, free to love, free to live at your maximum, free to be, to be all He wills you to be. It is the same kind of surrender that a loose wire, attached to nothing and creating nothing, makes when it surrenders itself to a dynamo. Now it throbs with energy, with light and power. It lives in living for something beyond itself. Paint surrenders itself to an artist and mere color becomes a beautiful picture. Marble surrenders itself to the sculptor and a mere block of expressionless marble becomes an almost living figure. Ink surrenders itself to the writer and mere fluid begins to throb with intelligence and passion.

The surrender which seems downward, laying down your arms, is actually a surrender upwards. It is a surrender to creative love. This is not acquiescence. It is cooperation with the power that raised Jesus from the dead—that power when surrendered to and cooperated with will raise us from a dead noncontributive life to a creative fruitful one. It is not the potter and the clay figure. Jesus never used that figure—for that figure is inert and mechanical rather than dynamic and willingly co-operative. In surrender you align your will to an almighty will, and you begin to do things you can't do, to accomplish the unaccomplishable, a suprise to yourself and others.

After the Second World War I was in a plane going out to India. The plane was to return with a cargo. I was the only passenger. The pilots asked me if I would like to see Baghdad from their seat. After we had passed Baghdad they asked me if I had ever run a plane. I never had. "Sit there and do what we tell you." There were two sets of white parallel lines in the indicator, one representing the plane and the other representing level or horizontal. The concern was to keep those two sets of lines coinciding. When those sets of lines coincided the plane went along evenly. I didn't have to understand anything about the intricate mechanisms involved—I had to keep those two sets of lines coinciding as one. When I did, all the power of those great four engines were behind this controlled evenness, and we went on with a maximum of speed and quiet.

The one business of human living is to keep our wills coinciding with the will of God in self-surrender and constant obedience. When we do, the sum total of reality is behind us, we have cosmic backing for our way of life. The bumps come when we get out of alignment with His will and purpose, when self-will takes over.

This reduces life to simplicity. If instead of self-surrender you undertake self-mortification, lopping off

34

here, lopping off there, suppressing here, suppressing there, you are tense and anxious and strained. The piety produced is a strained piety, strained hence drained. A man introduced his wife to me: "I'm introducing my wife to you. She is one of your 'rastling' Christians." She was. Her face was strained and anxious. Every organ of her body was tied up by that mental and spiritual anxiety.

A professor in a theological seminary scoffed before his class at a phrase in one of my books: "Let go and let God." It wasn't strenuous enough. He missed the point entirely. For the difference is a difference of standpoint; the unsurrendered self works out from its own motives and resources; the surrendered self works out from the motives and resources of Christ. Identified with Christ the surrendered are identified with His resources. They are His, because He is His. Paul puts it in these words: "To this end I am toiling strenuously with all the energy and power of Christ at work in me" (Col. 1: 29 NEB). His will and Christ's will were coinciding, and his energy and Christ's energy were also coinciding. This divine-human strenuous striving was not exhausting but exhilarating. You are doing everything for His sake and by His power. It is effortless striving. Those who talk about the strenuous life are usually talking about the strained life. But the surrendered are quietly creative and actually produce twice as much as the unsurrendered with all their fussy activity. Dr. Merton Rice puts it thus: "The hurrieder I go, the behinder I get." The unsurrendered have to increase their pace to cover the fact that they have lost the way. A missionary said it this way: "I've spent my time in running away from things." Unsurrendered, that missionary spent his time "in running," in running away from things. The surrendered spend their time in walking through things, in walking through problems, through responsibilities, through opportunities, through everything that comes up, walking confidently with all the energy and power at work in them. So the surrendered are the strenuous, the quietly and effectively and creatively strenuous. I say "the creatively strenuous," for we are made by the Creator for creation. When we cease to create we degenerate.

When we are surrendered to God, the Creator, and to Christ, the re-Creator, we are surrendered to creative love and hence are creative and fulfilled. We go singing on our way to our tasks and obligations and responsibilities.

The self is not canceled when surrendered. It is heightened. A plus is added to all we do and say and are, a divine plus.

But in all this is there no minus, is there no death, is it all life? No, there is a death, a death to the false life we have been living and to the false I we have built up. The false, unnatural world of sin and evil, the false self, organized around egoism, has to die. When Paul said: "I have been crucified with Christ," he meant that false world and that false self were crucified. He didn't mean his self, his real self was annihilated, canceled, for in the next breath he says: "it is no longer I who live." He was cleansed by the crucifixion of the false self, this body of death that had clung to him. A new man arose, God's man, and therefore he was alive—"it is no longer I who live." He was now alive to his fingertips, alive in every cell of his body and mind and spirit. He was alive! We never live until we have gone to our own funeral. Then we come back singing. The whole passage telling of Paul's burial and resurrection reads this way: "I have been crucified with Christ" (you have died to all the purposes in your life except the purposes of Christ), "I have been crucified *with* Christ; it is no longer I who live." Crucifixion with Christ is resurrection in yourself, you *live* and how! Everything within you and around you is alive! "It is no longer I who live, but Christ who lives in me"—your life is essentially the life of another. You have merged your interests and being in the life of another, "but Christ who lives in me." "And the life I now live in the flesh I live by faith in the Son of God," and this life is not vaguely spiritual, it is "in the flesh," operating in and through the material; "I live by faith in the Son of God," the pattern of my life is the Son of God, and the power of my life is the Son of God. He is both pattern and power. "Who loved me and gave himself for me"—that pattern is love and a self-giving love: "gave himself for me" (Gal. 2:20 RSV).

This passage is gloriously mixed—the human and divine intermingled, and yet the human is not lost in the divine and the divine not merged into the human. Each is separate and both are one. The end is communion, not identity, the most intimate communion possible or imaginable. Yet the communion is not senti-

37

mentality; it is a communion that has self-giving love for one another and for all.

To surrender to that kind of creative love, embodied in a person, is to surrender to the highest—in this universe or any other. In view of this possibility to surrender to your self, to pride, to lust, to the herd, to money, to resentments, to hate, to fear is not only bad, it is stupid. It is crime against ourselves and others. Surrender then is not a grudging compulsion but a happy yielding of ourselves to the love and goodness of God, to God himself.

So the self is not swamped, nor flattened out, nor tied up with restrictions—"I can't do this, I can't do that," —nor dominated over, but by complete obedience is completely free, free to live and love and create, to be at its best—His best.

The conception of "Oh to be nothing, just to lie at His feet, a broken and empty vessel, for the Master's service complete," is gone. You are not a "nothing," you are a something, a some one, with a plus added to all you do and say and are.

Now you "know yourself." You know yourself as a child of God, made in His image, now under redemption, and are being remade from a life of sin and self-idolatry into the image of the Son of God. "And we all, with unveiled face, beholding the glory of the Lord, are being changed into his likeness from one degree of glory to another" (II Cor. 3:18 RSV). Knowing that, I know my self. Until I know this destiny and am under its fulfillment, all my knowing is half-knowing, flickering candles of brief and partial insights, but not knowing my real destiny and possibilities. Is there anything higher in heaven or in earth or under the earth than to be "changed into his likeness?" If so, let men in East and West bring it out. It just isn't there to be brought out. The highest adjective descriptive of character in any language is the adjective Christlike.

"Life is not fair,"   "The Past is a prison,"
Said the Angel.   Said the Man.
"The future is a trap,"   "Love is too cautious,"
Said the Devil.   Said the Woman."
        "I have no answer,"
        Said God.   —Charles Angoff.

This is falsity itself. God has an answer: His answer is Christ, and to be Christlike is our destiny. If you do not know that answer and are not under that destiny, then you have exactly what these lines depict: Life is not fair; the future is a trap; the past is a prison; love is too cautious. If you haven't God's answer you come out to this pessimism. You come out to this dilemma: A man on television angrily said to another, "I don't know which would be worse, having to be with you or to be with myself." If you won't live with God you can't live with yourself, nor with anyone else.

All that pessimism about life and yourself and others drops away when you surrender to God. You have faith in God, in life, in people, and in destiny. You have faith and faith has you. You create faith. The author of those lines, if he meant what he said, didn't reveal the

39

angel, or the devil, or the man, or the woman, or God—
he revealed himself. He didn't hold pessimism, pessimism held him, he *was* pessimism. But when you surrender to God the sneer becomes a cheer, the snort becomes a shout, pessimism becomes possibility, life becomes alive.

"The only thing I wanted out of life was to get out of
it," said a friend, until he surrendered to Christ, and then
he believed in life for he belonged to Life.

The statement, "God appears in the life when the self
disappears," has to be amended. The self doesn't dis-
appear, it appears as surrendered and creative and adjusted, appears as its self because as His. His will is our
freedom, freedom to be and to become.

My spiritual home in which I have lived for many
years is this verse: "For all belongs to you; Paul, Apollos,
Cephas"—all great teachers—"the world, life, death"—
all great facts—"the present and the future"—all time—
"all belongs to you"—everything—"and you belong to
Christ, and Christ to God" (I Cor. 3:22, 23 Moffatt).
This verse reveals that if you belong to Christ all belongs
to you. This reverses the views of many who believe that
the Christian faith is a suppression, a denial of the will
to live. It is the will to acquiesce, to surrender, to be willing to be a nothing, it is the will to die. But if this verse
is true, then it is the mightiest affirmation imaginable of
the will to live: all great teachers, all great facts, all time,
all things belong to you, provided you belong to Christ.

All great teachers—Paul, Apollos, Cephas. The center
of the Christian faith is Jesus Christ. In Corinth they

had slipped off that center and had begun to be centered in good men, instead of the God-Man. You can exhaust good men, but you cannot exhaust the God-Man. Seminaries and individuals become Barthians, Bultmannians, Tillichites, and what not. Result? They become second-hand, live on quotation marks, their wells run dry. But you never exhaust Jesus Christ. The more you know, the more you know there is to be known. There is a surprise around every corner. Your horizons are cracking with novelty and popping with newness of insight and revelation. Besides, to center in good men instead of the God-man is to be divisive. Around Christ we are one, around Barth, Bultmann, Tillich we are not one—we are divided over them. But if you say: I belong to Christ and these teachers belong to me, anything good they have is mine, but I don't belong to them—then with your one point of the compass on Christ the other point can sweep as far into truth as possible. You are anchored—and free.

Then, the world, life, death—all great facts—belong to you. There is a world, built up by sin and evil, that does not belong to you. It is a false world. John says of that world: "Do not love the world or the things in the world. If any one loves the world, love for the Father is not in him. For all that is in the world, the lust of the flesh and the lust of the eyes and the pride of life, is not of the Father but is of the world. And the world passes away, and the lust of it; but he who does the will of God abides for ever" (I John 2:15-17 RSV). That world of the lust of the flesh, the lust of the eyes, and the pride of life is a false world, is not of the Father and will pass away. But the world of beauty, of art, of sunsets and sunrises, of pure love and the faces of little children does belong to you if you belong to Christ. I never saw the world until I saw its Creator, saw Him in reconciliation and redemption. Then suddenly the world became alive to me, trees clapped their hands, nature was alive, and my aliveness matched its aliveness and I, too, clapped my hands. I had to amend the words of a hymn: "the things of the world grow strangely dim in the light of His wonderful face," to "the things of the world grow strangely bright in the light of His wonderful face." The Christian's faith is false-world-denying, but not world-denying. The world belongs to him.

Life belongs to you—life belongs to you because you belong to Life. At one of my "listening posts," a time in the early morning when I don't ask for anything but listen to see if God has anything to say to me, He said to me: "You are mine, life is yours." I was startled and asked Him to repeat it. And He did: "You are mine, life is yours." That saying has been singing its way through my heart ever since: If I belong to Christ, life belongs to me; I can master it, rescue some good out of everything, good, bad, and indifferent. That statement was a "certificate guaranteeing adequacy" in any situation, in any condition, in any period of life. It is a universal guarantee that life is my servant, if I am His slave. Then I do not have to be concerned about this, that, or the other. I have one concern and only one—that I be His. Secure there, I am secure. Not that I am guaranteed to be free from sorrow, trouble, sickness, death. I know that these

42

four things will come to me. But I don't belong to them. I belong to Christ, these things belong to me, belong to me to make something out of them; not to bear them, but to use them. "You are mine, life is yours."

Death belongs to you if you belong to Jesus Christ, the deathless One. Someone writing about Petula Clark, the singer, said: "In her hit song 'Downtown' something overjoyed in her free and easy voice says goodbye to the painful past and turns the song into an emancipation proclamation:

> When you are alone, and life is making you lonely,
> You can always go—Downtown!
> When you've got worries all the noise and hurry
> Seems to help I know—Downtown! *

Of all the revelations of the superficiality of this age this is the most revealing. It is an emancipation proclamation from loneliness and worries to go downtown and mingle with the hurrying crowd! Concentrated loneliness and concentrated worries are to cure individual loneliness and worry! They may for a moment, for the crowd distracts your attention from the unhappy you; but when you get out of the distracting crowd and are back again with you, then nothing is cured, for you are not cured.

Besides, suppose illness and approaching death come

---

along and you can't go downtown—what then? You are
left alone with your misery, with you. Then you are like
the man in the Scriptures who had devils, "a man from
the city [who] dwelt in the tombs." The devils in him
were city devils! The devils of the city invaded him and
he went to the solitude of the tombs to get relief from
them, only to find he carried his loneliness and worries
within him, whether in solitude or in city. He ended up
dwelling in tombs—dwelling in tombs while alive. But
if you are in Christ you are not dwelling in tombs, alive
or so-called dead. If you are surrendered to Christ you
are surrendered to Life. Death then is your servant, the
servant that opens the door to fuller life. You conquer
death by using death.

All time belongs to you if you belong to Christ, the
present and the future. Many are not afraid of death,
but they are afraid of this thing called time. It leaves its
marks in greying hair and wrinkled skin. Then comes the
flight to arresting processes, the face-lifting, the cos-
metics and dyes, the makeup which becomes make-
believe. It's a losing battle, my sister, my brother! What,
then, are we to do? Welcome the coming and going of
time, for you do not belong to time, you belong to Christ
and He is the same yesterday, today and forever, the
unchanging, the unfading. He is not a sunset or evening
star, He is the bright and morning star, a sunrise! The
Scripture says that "the tree of life bears twelve manner
of fruit, each month having its own fruit." Can each
period of life, each month, have its own fruit and beauty?
I've found it so, I've found it so! "There is something

in the autumn that is native to my blood." When I am surrendered to Christ, autumn brings serenity, ripeness, calm, joy and expectancy, brings His everything. If His somethings have been wonderful, what will His everything be! The end will be better than the beginning and the middle, for the end has the beginning and the middle and the end in it, all three. And more than all three, a fresh beginning, with the experience of all three at my disposal. I'll be saved a lot of trial and error, for I know how life works; it works in His way. What a conclusion on which to begin the fresh beginning!

So surrender means not renunciation, but renunciation to realization. Now I know myself.

And now I can accept my self. I can accept it for it is an acceptable self, it is under redemption. It is not at the goal, but it is on the way. And the way of the Way seems good.

A girl, now converted and radiant, said, "I like the person I'm becoming." A Swedish woman in the "Morning of the Open Heart" said, "I don't like myself and I don't like others." She surrendered herself to Christ, and on the last day, "the Morning of the Overflowing Heart," she said: "I love everybody this morning and, strangely enough, I love myself." When you love Christ by self-surrender to Him, then you love others and you love your self. For the Christian faith teaches self-love: "Thou shalt love thy neighbor as thyself." You are to love yourself. To hate and reject and despise your self is just as bad as to hate and reject and despise others. When you surrender to Christ, all self-hate, all self-loath-

45

ing, all self-rejection drop away. How can you hate what He loves? How can you reject what He accepts? How can you look down on what He died for? You are no longer a person, you are "a person for whom Christ died." If He died for me, there must be something in me worth dying for. I am important, because I'm His.

So I can accept myself.

Now I can express myself. Paul says "For to me to live is Christ" (Phil. 1:21 RSV), therefore to express himself was to express Christ. To express this redeemed self is a witness to Him. So surrender to Christ saves you, on the one hand, from egotistic self-assertion, always wanting to occupy the center of attention, and, on the other hand, from shyness which is always shrinking and thinking, "what do they think of me?" It saves you from self-consciousness and from herd-consciousness because you have Christ-consciousness. You are not a worm, nor a wonder. You are the ordinary becoming the extraordinary, all due to Him. So you can be yourself because you are His self. You are free to be.

So you find self-realization through Christ-realization, no other way. If you meditate on your self being the Self, the divine Self, then this is not self-surrender but self-assertion. As such it is self-defeating. Those who try to realize themselves as the Divine Self must throw around themselves a lot of hocus-pocus as manifesting the divine Self. I was told by a disciple of one such swami: "He is divine; he can tell you anything." When I asked him a question to test his divinity he replied:

"My mind is tired." If his mind was a divine mind, why should it be tired?

When you are surrendered to Christ you don't have to keep up appearances to prove anything, to play a part; you have to be just yourself. You have to simply point to Him and say, "I am what I am by the grace of God." That points to another and releases you from self-consciousness. You are supernaturally natural.

So you can know yourself, can accept yourself, and can express yourself if you surrender yourself. No other way works. This one does. You fulfill psychology and you fulfill yourself.

3

Is God Cruel or Consistent in
Demanding Self-Surrender?

We must now go back to the Finnish reporter's question: "Why is God so cruel? Why does He demand so much of us?" In demanding self-surrender, is God being cruel or consistent? Is self-surrender only to be in the human or is it also in the divine? Does God demand something He doesn't do? Or is this demand really an offer, an offer to share what He Himself does? For God and man, is self-surrender the deepest law of the universe? Is it law that "whoever would save his life will lose it, and whoever loses his life . . . will find it?" (Matt. 16:25 RSV). And does this law hold good for God and man?

> By all that God requires of me,
> I know that He Himself must be.

God obeys every law He demands of us. And He especially obeys and illustrates the law of finding His life

48

by losing it. This principle is at the very heart of the universe. This verse vividly proclaims that fact: "the Lamb who is at the heart of the throne will be their shepherd and will guide them to the springs of the water of life" (Rev. 7:17 NEB). That phrase, "the Lamb who is at the heart of the throne," is the most important of any verse in Scripture, or in literature anywhere. What is at the heart of final power in the universe? That determines our view of the universe, and ultimately it determines our lives. Show me your gods and I will show you your men—show me what you think is at the heart of the universe and I will show you what will be at the heart of your conduct.

Call the roll of the answers of philosophy and religion as to what is at the heart of the throne of the universe, and what answers do we get? Justice, power, law, indifference, question mark, favoritism, something that cannot be wangled, the non-manipulatable, the ground of our being. Nothingness. Not one could rise to, or could dare think of, self-giving, sacrificial love, "the Lamb," being at the heart of the throne. That would be unthinkable, it could only come as revelation, and not as verbal revelation. The Word had to become flesh, we had to see it in the Lamb, God on a cross!

The unimaginable revelation is this: God not only redeems in terms of Jesus Christ, He rules in terms of Jesus Christ. The Lamb is at the heart of the throne, the throne and not merely the cross! Does God rule from a cross? Then the cross is final power and not only absolute goodness.

49

Is this a stray thought woven into the fabric of Christianity, or is it the warp and woof of the whole? This verse lets us see that it is at the very basis of the Christian faith, founded on what God does and not merely on what He commands: "Therefore, my brothers, I implore you by God's mercy to offer your very selves to him: a living sacrifice" (Rom. 12:1 NEB). The word "therefore" is the key word in this passage. It is the pivot upon which the whole epistle turns from doctrines to duties, from what God has done to what we are to do. And what has He done? The whole of the Epistle to the Romans up to the eighth chapter (the ninth, tenth, and eleventh chapters are a diversion) is an exposition of what God has done to redeem us. The following passage lets us see what He has done: "Christ died for us while we were yet sinners, and that is God's own proof of his love towards us. And so, since we have now been justified by Christ's sacrificial death, . . . For if, when we were God's enemies, we were reconciled to him through the death of his Son, . . . now that we are reconciled, shall we be saved by his life. But that is not all: We also exult in God through our Lord Jesus, through whom we have now been granted reconciliation" (Rom. 5:8-11 NEB). Also: "He did not spare his own Son, but surrendered him for us all; and with this gift how can he fail to lavish upon us all he has to give?" (Romans 8:32 NEB.) Put with the above this: "God was in Christ reconciling the world to himself" (II Cor. 5:19 NEB). Put these passages together and they spell out the astonishing news: God was in Christ reconciling the world unto himself.

So self-surrender is at the very heart of God and is at the very heart of all His attitudes and actions. When He asks us to surrender ourselves He is asking us to fulfill the deepest thing in Himself and the deepest thing in us. It is not only the deepest in God—it is also the highest in God. God was never higher than when He gave Himself for us. If there were a cosmic newspaper announcing: GOD THE CREATOR OF THE UNIVERSE GIVES HIMSELF TO REDEEM A PLANET CALLED EARTH!—the universe would gasp in astonishment, that would be news, Good News. It would be more than good news, it would set the standard for life in the universe. We must do what God does, surrender ourselves. If we do that we are in harmony with the universe. The sum total of reality is behind us, sustains us, furthers us, approves of us; we have cosmic backing. If we go against what God does, make ourselves the center of life, then we are running athwart the universe; we have nothing behind us except our lonely wills; we are estranged and out of harmony with the universe and ourselves. We have saved our lives and have lost them.

So Paul says: "Therefore, . . . I implore you by God's mercy to offer your very selves to him: a living sacrifice." "Therefore" puts you and God in alignment. His will and your will coincide. And when this happens, then His power and your power coincide. His power is yours, for His purpose is yours.

Why does Paul say: I implore by God's mercy? Why by God's mercy? Is he implying: God have mercy on

51

you if you don't? I think so, for life says so! All the problems of human living come out of self-centered living. Center yourself on your self and you won't like yourself. And no one else will like you. A psychologist says: "It's a million chances to one that the self-centered are unpopular." With whom? First, with themselves. They do as they like and then don't like the self they are expressing. I asked in a youth meeting: "Have you ever seen a happy self-centered person?" At the close a youth came up to me and said: "I'm your exception. I'm completely self-centered and I'm completely happy." I replied: "Well, enjoy it as long as you can, for it won't last long." His knees buckled, literally buckled. He knew he was whistling to keep up his courage. He was fulfilling this verse: "In my mouth it did taste sweet as honey; but when I swallowed it my stomach turned sour" (Rev. 10:10 NEB). To be a self-centered person tastes sweet in the mouth. It makes you feel good that you have had your way, initially good, the ego has triumphed. But when you try to digest self-centeredness the stomach turns sour. You are not made to be the center of your universe. On that basis none of your sums add up. You are made for outgoing love, not ingrown self-preoccupation. Your stomach and your relationships turn sour. Neither can you as a person digest it, nor can your relationships.

This law of saving your life by losing it is not based on God's whim, nor even upon God's will—it is based on God's character. That is the way God is, and that is the way God acts, and if we act otherwise we are at cross-purposes with God and consequently get hurt, get hurt automatically. For you cannot be at cross-purposes with reality and get away with it. You don't break this law, you break yourself upon it. It registers its consequences within you. You are paid in your own person the fitting wage of such perversion, the perversion of making yourself God instead of surrendering to God.

So "I implore you by God's mercy" can mean: God have mercy on you if you don't surrender to God. This surrender to God is not merely a religious doctrine, it is a life demand. The rest of Rom. 12:1 says that offering "your very selves to him: a living sacrifice" is "the worship offered by mind and heart." Note "mind," or as the King James Version says, "your reasonable service." To surrender to God is "reasonable," is the sensible thing to do. From the moment you surrender to God, life takes on meaning, goal, purpose, a sense of going somewhere worthwhile—life adds up to sense.

Hammarskjöld, the able general secretary of the United Nations, in his book, *Markings*, says: "You will find that, thus subordinated, your life will receive from Life all its meaning, irrespective of the conditions given you for its realization. You will find that the freedom of the continual farewell, the hourly self-surrender, gives to your experience of reality the purity and clarity which signify—self-realization" (p. 130). Five years later he tells how he personally surrendered to God: "But at some moment I did answer Yes to Someone—or Something—and from that hour I was certain that existence is meaningful and that, therefore, my life, in self-surrender,

53

had a goal" (p. 205). From that moment life was "reasonable"—it added up to sense, not nonsense.

The most sensible moment of your life, and the most sensible thing you ever do is the moment when you say yes to someone, when you surrender to him.

Now note the next step in that passage: "Adapt yourselves no longer to the pattern of this present world." The tyranny of the herd pressure on the individual is broken, you are no longer herd-centered when you are surrendered to God. "Everybody does it" is replaced by, "This is what He would have me do." You are delivered from herd-domination, but you are not unsocial, withdrawn. "Delivering thee from the people to whom I now send thee"—delivered from the people, you can now serve them. You cannot serve people unless you are delivered from them. If you always wonder, "what do they think of me" you are not free to serve people. Self-surrender delivers you from surrender to the herd, and that is a blessed deliverance. There is another deliverance by self-surrender: "But let your mind be remade and your whole nature thus transformed." Here the mind is "remade"; it is not a mind that is engrossed in thinking about itself, its wants and desires, its hurts and its slights, its self-pity and resentments. It is a mind that is circling around a new center, Christ, therefore thinking His thoughts, and therefore healthy, constructive, creative thoughts. Such thinking helps to transform your whole nature and outlook: "and your whole nature thus transformed."

Self-surrender delivers you from self-preoccupation, herd-preoccupation, and preoccupation with off-center

thinking. Therefore "your whole nature" is "thus transformed."

The rest of the passage in Rom. 12:1, 2 ends this way:
"Then you will be able to discern the will of God, and to
know what is good, acceptable, and perfect." You try it,
and the moment you try it you go through three stages:
Why this is *good*—it has the feeling of being good and
leading to the good; I am adjusted to God and myself
and life; moreover it is *acceptable*—it fits me, body,
mind, and spirit. I am at home in it; and, finally, it is
perfect—I wouldn't change a thing about it except to be
more perfectly adjusted to this glorious perfection.

Self-surrender, then, is to surrender to the perfect person and the perfect purposes of the God who illustrates
in Himself the wonder of self-surrender.

But is this self-surrender in God a fact or a fiction? It
is a fact. But we could never have seen it, for He is an
eternal Spirit, unless we had seen it in the incarnation—
in Jesus Christ. If Jesus is the human life of God, then
the attitudes and acts of Jesus are the attitudes and acts
of God. He is the Word of surrender become flesh.
Fortunately we see in Him the crisis hour of self-surrender
in the episode described in John 12:20-33 when the
Greeks came and said to Philip: "Sir, we should like to
see Jesus" (NEB). This precipitated an amazing soul
crisis in Jesus: "The hour has come for the Son of Man
to be glorified. In truth, in very truth I tell you, a grain
of wheat remains a solitary grain unless it falls into the
ground and dies; but if it dies, it bears a rich harvest."
Why should a simple interview by Greeks precipitate a

crisis, a crisis in which dying or not dying seemed to be the issue? Was the matter the Greeks brought up something like this: Sir, if you go on the way your face is set, these Jews will kill you. Don't go on to Jerusalem, come to Athens. Put your marvellous message of the Kingdom of God through Greek philosophy and culture. It will thus spread through the world. You will gain your ends by becoming our teacher, our beloved teacher and philosopher. Don't go to Jerusalem and die, come to Athens and live, live long and honored.

The issue was self-saving or self-losing, a philosopher's chair or a cross. This is not farfetched, for the Jews once said: "Will he go to the Dispersion among the Greeks, and teach the Greeks?" (John 7:35.) Tradition says that the king of Edessa asked Jesus to come to Edessa.

Jesus reveals the deep soul crisis: "The man who loves himself is lost . . . Now my soul is in turmoil. Shall I say, 'Father, save me from this hour?' " (Margin.) "No, it was for this that I came to this hour. Father, glorify Thy name." He would not rationalize or compromise, He would face it. He would surrender to God: "Father, glorify Thy name." He gave a blank check to God signed in His own blood. He knew it was Jerusalem and its cross for Him. But He also knew that behind that self-surrender to a cross lay ultimate power and ultimate victory: "Now is the hour of judgment for this world; now shall the Prince of this world be driven out. And I shall draw all men to myself when I am lifted up from the earth. This he said to indicate the kind of death he was to die." The self would fall into the ground and die and bear a rich harvest. He aligned Himself with self-giving instead of self-saving. And in doing so He revealed the deepest thing in the heart of God—self-sacrifice, the Lamb at the heart of the throne. God rules by self-giving, He rules from a cross.

When Peter made the great confession at Caesarea Philippi that Jesus is "the Christ, the Son of the Living God," it was no mere chance that the confession was made there. For at Caesarea Philippi was a white grotto where an image of Caesar was worshiped as God. Is the power back of the universe a Caesar-like power—force? Or is the power back of the universe a Christlike power —suffering love? They knew who He was, now He would let them know what was at the heart of being "the Messiah, the Son of the living God." "From that time Jesus began to make it clear to his disciples that he had to go to Jerusalem, and there to suffer from the elders, chief priests, and lawyers; to be put to death and to be raised again on the third day" (Matt. 16:21 NEB). Peter "took him by the arm and began to rebuke him: . . . 'No, Lord, this shall never happen to you.'" Peter thought that the Messiah would be a self-assertive Messiah, would conquer Caesar and the world—by force. He was appalled, all his dreams of world dominion were crashing, so he took Jesus "by the arm" and rebuked Him. He tried to hold Jesus to Peter's dream of power. And then came the shattering reply of Jesus to Peter: "Away with you, Satan; you are a stumbling-block to me. You think as men think, not as God thinks" (Matt. 16:21-23). In other words, Jesus revealed that in taking

57

the cross He was revealing the very thought of God, for He was revealing the very nature of God. Peter was still on the self-assertive side instead of in the self-surrender side, so Jesus had to call Peter a "Satan." Harsh? He had to be, for the greatest issue of the universe was at stake: What is God like? Caesar? Or the self-giving Christ? Is force or love at the heart of the universe? When Peter rejected the idea of suffering love he was a "Satan," for that is how Satan became Satan, Lucifer become proud and self-assertive. "I watched how Satan fell, like lightning out of the sky," said Jesus. When did He say that? The seventy came back jubilant: "In your name, Lord, even the devils submit to us." Note: "submit to us." Using the name of Jesus to get devils to "submit to us." Self at the center even when casting out devils. So Jesus had to warn them of how Satan fell—by putting himself at the center.

One would have thought, when the disciples, through Peter, made the confession that Jesus was the Christ, the Son of the living God, that everything would fall into place after this, would be the pivot around which everything would revolve. For three years they were uncertain as to who He was—man or incarnate God? Now it was clear and everything would come out clear. But after this confession nothing was done right in the rest of the chapter. They went from blunder to blunder, from clash to clash. Note the clashes:

1. Individual disciple with individual disciple. "A dispute arose among them: which of them was the greatest?" (Luke 9:46.) As a group they could not get along

58

with one another—there was an inner struggle for place and power.

2. A group of disciples clashing with a group of disciples. " 'Master,' said John, 'we saw a man casting out devils in your name, but as he is not one of us we tried to stop him' " (Luke 9:49). Not one of us—the group clash, group against group.

3. Race clashing with race. "They set out and went into a Samaritan village to make arrangements for him; but the villagers would not have him because he was making for Jerusalem. When the disciples James and John saw this they said, 'Lord, may we call down fire from heaven to burn them up?' But he turned and rebuked them, and they went on to another village" (Luke 9:52-56). Here was a race clash—Jew against Samaritan.

4. Individuals clashing with their own selves. (a) "As they were going along the road a man said to him, 'I will follow you wherever you go.' Jesus answered: 'Foxes have their holes, the birds their roosts; but the Son of Man has nowhere to lay his head' " (Luke 9:57-59). Jesus saw the man was looking for contradictory things, he wanted to follow Christ and to follow comfort. He was out of harmony with himself. (b) "To another he said, 'Follow me,' but the man replied, 'Let me go and bury my father first,' Jesus said, 'Leave the dead to bury their dead; you must go and announce the kingdom of God' " (Luke 9:59-60). Evidently the father was not lying dead at home, but the man wanted to go home and stay around till his father did die, so that he might give him a proper funeral to keep up the family name and

prestige, and incidentally that he might get a part of the father's inheritance, which he probably would not have received had he followed Jesus then. Here was a clash between following Jesus, and the desire to keep up the family status by a becoming funeral and get a part of the inheritance for himself. Mixed up with clashing desires. (c) "Yet another said, 'I will follow you, sir; but let me first say goodbye to my people at home.' To him Jesus said, 'No one who sets his hand to the plow and then keeps looking back is fit for the kingdom of God'." (Luke 9:61-62). Here was a man with a backward look, looking back to note how much he had given up to follow Jesus. He was "Mr. Facing-both-ways." He wanted to follow Jesus, in the present and the future, but he also wanted to cling to the past, saying to himself, "Look how much I have given up to follow Jesus." Self-surrender mingled with self-pity.

Here were four basic disharmonies: 1. Individual disciple clashing with individual disciple of the same group. Self-assertion can be in the individual. 2. Group clashing with group—a group following Jesus clashing with another group following Jesus. Self-assertion can be in the group. 3. Race against race—Jew against Samaritan. Self-assertion can be in the race—my race, right or wrong. 4. Individuals at clash with themselves as individuals. (a) One wanting Christ and comfort, incompatibles. (b) Another wanting to keep up the family name through a large funeral for his father and at the same time wanting to get an inheritance for himself. In either case, it was for himself. (c) Another wanting to cling to the past with a backward look: Look how much I am re-nouncing—self-surrender with self-piety.

The result of all this is a moral and spiritual impotence: "I asked your disciples to cast it out, but they could not" (Luke 9:40). Why could the disciples not cast out the devil from the boy? Because the boy had a better case of demon-possession than they had of God-possession. And the reason for the faint God-possession was that in each case they were still on the self-centered basis. They thought "as men thought"—self-saving, not self-losing. They knew who Jesus was—the Messiah, the Son of God—but did not grasp what was the center of His being the Son of God—self-losing. So He and they lived side by side in two different worlds, the world of self-saving and the world of self-losing. He had the key; they didn't. Through storm and opposition and hate and betrayal He always came out on the right side of things. They fumbled this business of living. Fumbled, until in the ten days in the Upper Room they got to the end of themselves, learned His secret, surrendered their very selves, laid hold on God's highest gift, the Holy Spirit, His all for their all. Then timid believers became irressistible apostles. They now had the secret—self-surrender.

The episode at Caesarea Philippi teaches us this: It is not enough to know that Jesus is the Christ, the Son of the living God. That knowledge did not transform the disciples, it left them going from blunder to blunder, every relationship awry. We say, knowledge is power, but it isn't power unless it leads to self-committal. Unless you surrender to the person of Jesus, you do not know the power of Jesus.

There is another incident that throws light on Jesus, revealing in His own person the nature of God as self-surrendered, self-giving love.

Jesus knew that his hour had come and he must leave this world and go to the Father. He had always loved his own who were in the world, and now he was to show the full extent of his love. The devil had already put it into the mind of Judas son of Simon Iscariot to betray him. During supper, Jesus, well aware that the Father had entrusted everything to him, and that he had come from God and was going back to God, rose from table, laid aside his garments, and taking a towel, tied it around him. Then he poured water into a basin, and began to wash his disciples' feet and to wipe them with the towel (John 13:1-5 NEB).

This washing of His disciples' feet, including Judas and including him after he had decided to betray Him, was an astonishing revelation of the basis of His humility. Jesus, well aware that the Father had entrusted everything to Him, knelt and washed His disciples' feet. In the consciousness of having "everything" in His power He did the lowliest thing possible. The consciousness of greatness was the secret of His humility. Those who are linked to themselves in self-centeredness dare not be humble, lest they give away their sense of insecurity and shallowness. So they seek for first places, prominence, heading the procession, attention to outwardly bolstering up their inward sense of inferiority.

The unsurrendered ego is always boastful, always bidding for attention, always recounting its greatness. Only the Incarnate God, conscious that everything was His, would dare stoop to wash His disciples' feet at the moment when an impending humiliation—the cross—was just ahead. This was compounding humiliation. But this is the point: having surrendered to God, He dared to surrender to man, to man, at his best in the person of His disciples, and to man at his worst in the person of His crucifiers.

He could throw to the winds all self-bolstering and all self-boasting and all self-saving. He was free, free to rise above everything and be conqueror in everything. Possessing all through self-surrender He now was free to conquer all. His inward position was this: Having died by self-surrender, what can death now do to me? I've already died by choice. Humiliation cannot hurt me, for I've already humiliated myself.

That is the secret of freedom for God and man. God the Creator was free to become man, the creature, because He was fulfilling the deepest law of the universe: saving his life by losing it. The servant of all becomes the greatest of all. That applies to God Incarnate and man.

Jesus was not a moralist, imposing a moral code. He was a revealer of the nature of reality. First, the revealer of the nature of God—God is self-surrendered, self-giving love. Second, the revealer of the nature of the universe. He seldom used the imperative, almost never the subjunctive, almost entirely the indicative. This was and still is His teaching. When He finished the Sermon on the Mount, His hearers "were astonished at his teaching, for he taught them as one who had authority, and not as their scribes" (Matt. 7:28, 29 RSV). With authority He taught them the law of self-surrender.

Jesus finished this episode of washing the disciples' feet with these words: "After washing their feet and taking his garments again, he sat down. 'Do you understand,' he asked, 'what I have done for you? You call me "Master" and "Lord," and rightly so, for that is what I am. Then if I, your Lord and Master, have washed your feet, you also ought to wash one another's feet'" (John 13:12-14 NEB). Note the change of the order: "You call me 'Master' (literally, Teacher) and 'Lord' . . . Then if I, your Lord and Master" (Teacher). They were saying, He is primarily Teacher and Lord. No, said Jesus. I am primarily your Lord and Teacher. That change was important, vitally important. Jesus is not primarily Teacher —He is primarily Lord. Self-surrender to Jesus Christ as Lord is the primary emphasis in the Christian faith. For Christianity is not a philosophy or a moralism to be learned. It is a Lord to be surrendered to and to be obeyed. If He is not your Lord, He is not your Teacher. He teaches those who obey Him, and only those who obey Him. We know as much as we are willing to practice and no more. The New Testament speaks of those who ever learning never come to the knowledge of the truth. Why do they never come to the knowledge of the truth? Because they were ever learning and never obeying. We learn as we obey, and in no other way.

So it was no mere chance that the earliest Christian creed was "Jesus is Lord," not "Jesus is Teacher." "If thou wilt confess with thy mouth that 'Jesus is Lord' . . . thou shalt be saved." "No man can say 'Jesus is Lord,' except by the Holy Spirit." The phrase 'Jesus is Lord' in both places is in quotation marks, showing it was used as the earliest Christian confession, the earliest Christian creed. If "Jesus is Lord" was the earliest Christian creed, then self-surrender to Jesus is the earliest Christian attitude and practice.

But through the centuries Christendom has let the disciples' order: "You call me 'Master' and 'Lord'" slip back into belief and practice. If you can repeat the creeds and the catechism, you are ready for baptism and church membership. Christianity is a proposition to be repeated instead of a person to be surrendered to. That simple change of order has been and is the most impoverishing thing that has ever crept into our faith. If we accept Jesus as Teacher, the self is not necessarily touched, but if you accept Jesus as Lord, then the self is touched, fundamentally so. It is surrendered. It abdicates—Jesus is Lord! Until you are surrendered you are a "self-ian;" when you are surrendered you are a "Christian," a Christian.

When some psychiatrists heard about the radiance of Mary Webster they thought it might be a neurotic radiance, so they suggested that she should be psychoanalyzed. I wrote to her half-jokingly telling her what the psychiatrists suggested. Her reply: "Why do they want to psychoanalyze me? I have no problems. Do they think

I'm off on religion? I'm not religious, I am His." That phrase: "I am not religious, I am His," is the dividing line between the two types: "Teacher and Lord" and "Lord and Teacher." In His being primarily "Teacher" you are religious; in His being primarily "Lord" you are His, you are a Christ-ian, a Christian. One is adsorption and the other is absorption. In adsorption you are like charcoal, holding particles on the outside; in absorption you are like a sponge, the particles permeating the very nature of the sponge. So there are ad-Christians, those who cling to Jesus on the outside, the unsurrendered; and there are ab-Christians, those who are permeated with Jesus, the surrendered.

A compelling passage which puts the principle and practice of self-surrender at the very heart of the divine is the following:

For the divine nature was his from the first; yet he did not think to snatch at equality with God, but made himself nothing, assuming the nature of a slave. Bearing the human likeness, revealed in human shape, he humbled himself, and in obedience accepted even death—death on a cross. Therefore God raised him to the heights and bestowed on him the name above all names, that at the name of Jesus every knee should bow—in heaven, on earth, and in the depths—and every tongue confess, "Jesus Christ is Lord," to the glory of God the Father (Phil. 2:6-11 NEB).

Now note the steps down: (1) "For the divine nature was his from the first." (2) "Yet he did not think to snatch at equality with God." (3) "But made himself nothing." (4) "Assuming the nature of a slave." (5) "He humbled himself." (6) "In obedience accepted even death." (7) "Death on a cross." There were seven steps down—from the throne to the cross. No greater self-giving than that can be imagined.

Now note the seven steps up: (1) "Therefore God raised him" (2) "To the heights." (3) "Bestowed on him the name above all names." (4) "That at the name of Jesus every knee should bow." (5) "In heaven, on earth, and in the depths." (6) "And every tongue confess, 'Jesus Christ is Lord.'" (7) "To the glory of God the Father."

There are two principles at work here, the principles of self-losing and of self-finding. The first principle is firmly planted in the nature of the divine. This is what God is and what God does. He gives, not marginally, His blessings here, His blessings there—He gives Himself. And He gives Himself not marginally, renouncing here, renouncing there; He gives Himself to a cross. That is the ultimate in surrender, in losing life.

The second principle at work here, the principle of self-finding, is also firmly planted in the nature of the divine: God takes His own medicine, obeys His own law of losing His life and finding it by losing it. He goes from a cross to a throne, every knee shall bow and every tongue confess "Jesus Christ is Lord" in universal homage. And this does not demean God; it is done "to the glory of God the Father." The God of the scars becomes the God of the stars.

A God like that can have my heart without reservation

or qualification. A nail-pierced hand holds the sceptre of the universe, and my knees bend before Him. If God did not have nail-pierced hands, I would not be interested in Him; a God who doesn't care, doesn't count. If, as Baron von Hügel says, "a Christian is one who cares," then the Christian God is also one who cares—and how!

If self-surrender is at the heart of the universe, at the heart of God, then, when Jesus apparently demands of us to offer our very selves a living sacrifice, the demand turns out not to be a demand but an offer. He offers us the privilege of doing what He is doing, and self-surrender turns out to be self-realization. You find yourself as you lose yourself.

Alongside this method of self-realization by self-surrender, the other methods of self-realization by trying to realize one's self as God seem tawdry. You sit and meditate and affirm yourself as God. But that is self-defeating for it is self-assertion, self-assertion of the crassest kind, man asserting himself as God. No wonder it never works. It can't work. For man is a man and not God, a creature and not the Creator.

But man is invited to be like God in self-surrender. And when he does he finds himself, not as God, but in communion with God at God's highest point, self-surrender. If the attempt to realize the self as the Self, as God, comes out of India and ends in futility, then something more wonderful has also come out of India. Mahatma Gandhi was asked: "If you were given the power to remake the world, what would you do first?"

He replied: "I would pray for power to renounce that power." He saw with rare insight that for him to assert the power to remake the world would end in his being a vast self-asserting autocrat. He preferred to be a self-giving servant. In this he rises in our love and admiration and in his influence upon us.

Jesus, knowing how outer titles influence inner attitudes, told His disciples of three titles they were not to use: "But you are not to be called 'rabbi,' for One is your teacher, and you are all brothers; you are not to call anyone 'father' on earth, for One is your heavenly Father; nor must you be called 'leaders,' for One is your leader, even the Christ. He who is greatest among you must be your servant. Whoever uplifts himself will be humbled, and whoever humbles himself will be uplifted" (Matt. 23:8-12 Moffatt). These titles express attitudes—all of them self-assertive. The "teachers" are those who feel that because they have a degree and a position of teacher, they necessarily are raised. Laotse, the Chinese sage, said: "Wise men are never scholars and scholars are never wise men." Exaggerated, but often true. The "fathers" are those who, by reason of experience and years, stand upon that pinnacle and take the attitude toward the younger generation: "Listen, wisdom is now speaking." They feel they have earned the right to authority, because, having lived long, they assume they necessarily have lived well. It doesn't necessarily follow. There is such a thing as a young fool, and also an old fool. Some in old age suffer from the hardening of the arteries, but more seriously from the hardening of the categories. A woman said in one of our meetings: "I'm about to jell into the kind of person I don't want to be." Some have already jelled!

The "leaders" have the attitude of, "I lead, you follow, fall in behind me." In spite of this warning from Jesus about being called leaders, we have encouraged this mentality in the Christian Church: "Classes for Training in Leadership," "How to Be a Leader," etc. Out of that mentality, do we produce leaders? Hardly. We produce fussy managers of other people. Our young people are exhorted on graduation day: "Now go out and be leaders." So they step out from graduation halls and say to the world: "I'm a leader, fall in behind me." And they are surprised that the world doesn't. And it doesn't. Why? Because it is off-track, running against the moral law: "He that exalteth himself shall be humbled."

Two men were on an Indian platform, one a man who was a religious politician, pulling wires, manipulating men and situations, all in his own interest. The other was Sadhu Sunder Singh who had lost his life in lowly service, wanting nothing except to present his Lord. When the first man spoke he shook himself, but not us. The more emphatic, the less effective he became. Inwardly we were saying, "Oh, yeah." When Sadhu Sunder Singh spoke we were all eyes, all ears—and all response. He had no outer position, no outer authority, but he held us like a vice, with the consent of all our inner beings. He was the embodiment both of self-losing and of self-finding.

On a monument to an Indian maharaja there were four

lines of titles. I turned to a friend and said: "They shall call his name Jesus." I cannot remember one of the maharaja's titles, or even his name. But the name of Jesus is not written on a monument, it is plowed into our very beings.

In a woman's meeting in India two women were rivals for the place of chairman. As they sat on each side of the retiring chairman one pulled her chair a little forward; the other noting it did the same. Then the first pulled her chair forward again and her rival matched it. This continued till they were on the edge of the platform. The audience seeing what was happening began to smile, then titter, then laugh. The two women went over the edge, into oblivion. The audience chose someone else as chairman.

Since all three of these attitudes, teachers, fathers, and leaders, were self-assertive and hence could not be christianized, what name was suitable and available? He names it: "He who is greatest among you must be your servant." "Servant" was the one name with which He could entrust them. The difference was very profound: the first three were self-centered and self-assertive and the last was self-losing.

Then what happens? A strange thing: "the servant of all" becomes "the greatest of all." "He that humbleth himself shall be exalted." And that does happen. Democracy, the highest form of government, when it chooses its leaders calls them "prime minister," first servant. The servant of all becomes the greatest of all. Moreover, if the prime minister instead of serving the

71

people begins to serve himself, using the office for his own ends, then the verdict is rendered in the ballot box —out he goes. "And great was the fall thereof."

If the only safe title for a Christian is "servant," is there no place for ambition in the Christian faith? Someone raised that question in a service club: "Then there is no place for a successful businessman in the Christian faith?" I reminded him that he belonged to a "service club," not a "self club." Why did they repudiate one and adopt the other? Because they saw, faintly or vividly, that the servant of all becomes the greatest of all.

There is a place for ambitious people in the Christian faith and there are degrees of greatness. "He who would be great among you shall be the servant of all"—to serve greatly makes you great. "He who would be first of all let him be slave of all." To be first of all let him go deeper in self-giving, let him be slave of all. Servant—great; slave —first. You go up to the degree that you go down. Then comes the highest and greatest of all: "The Son of man who gives his life as a ransom." So the degrees are these: "Servant" means great; "slave" means first; and "the Son of man who gives His life as a ransom" is the highest and greatest of all. Be like Him and the progress in greatness is infinite. The door is open upward as we go down the ladder of lowly self-giving.

This is the most astonishing revelation to greatness ever made, and the most beneficial to everybody concerned. For if you take this attitude you benefit the served and you benefit the server, you benefit everybody. But if you take the opposite attitude and become self-grasping you hurt society and you hurt yourself, both society and you yourself are impoverished.

To sum up this chapter: The principle and practice of self-surrender, self-losing to self-finding, is inherent in God and in man. If God should violate it He wouldn't be God, and if man violates it he wouldn't be man.

4

Is Self-Surrender Inherent in Nature?

We have seen that self-surrender is inherent in God and inherent in man and is the theme of the Scriptures. What has Nature to say?

A scientist has said: "God's method in nature is evolution and God's method in man is Christianity." In evolution the usual interpretation is that nature is red in tooth and claw; it is a survival of the fittest in terms of the sharpest tooth and claw; it is self against the rest. How can that process be God's method in nature?

But this interpretation of evolution as self against the rest is only one side of evolution. There is another side and Kropotkin has interpreted it in his thesis, "The Struggle for the Life of Others." Darwin's interpretation of lower nature as self against the rest was a half-truth, and when it was applied as the method of survival among man it has brought us to the greatest crisis in human history. The nations began to sharpen their national "tooth and claw," began to pile up armaments, discovered the atomic bomb and now have sufficient power to destroy themselves and everybody else. It has brought us to the brink of total disaster. We will have to find a method of survival that will save us from this "fruit"— total annihilation. "The law of mutual aid" is the method of survival in lower nature and among men. The law of mutual aid in parenthood is at the very basis of nature. Take that out and there would be no nature to survive.

The oldest living thing upon our planet is the giant Sequoia tree. It has survived for six reasons: (1) It is straight. It works with the law of gravitation and not against it. Were it crooked the law of gravitation would have pulled it down. (2) It puts out a supporting outer root to straighten if it it tends to lean. (3) It has an acid in its bark which the little borers don't like. It keeps sound within. (4) If a calamity strikes it, like a forest fire, and leaves a wound, it throws scar tissue around it. It has the power of self-healing. (5) If the top is knocked off by a lightning bolt it refuses to stop growing, it puts up a new top. (6) The trees live in clumps and their roots intertwine; they hold one another up if a storm strikes them, they are a society of mutual aid. As a society of mutual aid they illustrate the oldest and most important law of survival in nature and in man.

The five levels of life illustrate the principle of self-surrender to the higher kingdom: the mineral kingdom, the vegetable kingdom, the animal kingdom, the kingdom of man, the kingdom of God. Each of these kingdoms may violate that law of self-surrender to the higher kingdom, decide to remain on its own level, believing that there is nothing beyond itself. The mineral kingdom may decide that there is nothing beyond itself, that life stops with the mineral. But the vegetable kingdom knows there is a higher life than that of the mineral. So the vegetable, the animal, the kingdom of man may each in turn decide there is nothing beyond itself. When we come to the kingdom of man, man may deliberately decide that he represents life at its highest, nothing beyond—life is humanism, man is God.

But in all ages, among all peoples, man seems to be pressed upon from above by a higher kingdom, the kingdom of God. That pressure from above awakens man to aspiration, to prayer, a kind of nostalgia, a homesickness for God. Man finds himself between two kingdoms, the kingdom of the animal and the kingdom of God. The kingdom of the animal stands for self against the rest, and the kingdom of God for the divine Self for the sake of the rest; one is red in tooth and claw and the other is red with the blood of its own self-sacrifice for the sake of the rest; one is mutual slaughter and the other is mutual aid; one is life animated by the hunger motive modified here and there by the love motive, the other is animated by the love motive only. Man can decide to yield himself to the higher or to the lower—he can be born from above, or born from below.

How can a man pass from the kingdom of man to the kingdom of God? By trying harder, by seeking through knowledge to arrive? None of those. The higher kingdom

76

must come down. Jesus is that divine coming. He says to us: "Cease trying. Surrender to me." We do it. We know not how, but we are taken up, up, transformed and transfigured, born from above, "there is a new creation, old things have passed away, behold they have become new." We are part of a new order, the kingdom of God.

A woman came to one of our Ashrams and said in the "Open Heart" session: "I've come here to get my self off my own hands." The self on your own hands is a problem and a pain; in the hands of God it is a possibility and a power. The self on your own hands may be a very religious self—it makes no difference, it is destructive, religiously so!

The principle of losing your life to find it again is seen in the three stages of life: dependence—the childhood stage; independence—the adolescent stage; interdependence—the mature stage. The childhood stage is where the child depends upon the parents for everything, for food, clothing, guidance, sympathy, love. Then comes the adolescent stage, the stage of independence. The adolescent boy and girl want to make their own decisions, be persons in their own rights, have room around their own personalities to grow. It is a difficult stage for parents and for adolescents. Some parents want to make all the decisions for the adolescents, and some adolescents want to make all the decisions without regard to the parents. It is a period of strain, for it involves a clash of egos. Someone has defined adolescence as "a period of temporary insanity." I quoted that in a woman's meeting, and a woman came up at the close and said: "That was the most hopeful thing you said, for I thought it was permanent." I didn't blame her, for I had tried to deal with her adolescent boy, and he was the most tied-up, cantankerous bit of humanity I had ever seen.

But whether we like it or not, we all have to go through that stage of gaining our own independence, some go through it painfully and destructively and some more or less naturally, according to the degree of self-centeredness.

Then we come to the third stage, interdependence, the stage of maturity. After we gain independence, we find it is not what it is cracked up to be. We are not independent. We marry and hence are not independent; have children and are still less independent; we are citizens of a state, a nation, a world—we have to relate to all of these, we have to become interdependent. In the stage of interdependence we sovereignly take our independence and surrender it to a higher entity, the individual to the home, the citizen to the state, nation, world, to the kingdom of God. In each case we surrender sovereignty and find a higher fellowship, in the home, the nation, the world, in the kingdom. To the degree that we do that we become mature. To the degree that we refuse that surrender to the higher relationship, we remain immature. We become mature persons by self-surrender. So self-surrender is written, not merely in the Bible, it is written into the very nature of our relationships and hence inescapable.

If a person refuses to make that surrender of independence to become interdependent, he automatically remains adolescent, refuses to grow up. He may be sixteen or sixty, but he is still adolescent.

Psychology, when it is true and not abnormal psychology, bears out this necessity of self-surrender to something higher than yourself if you are to find your self. The psychologists say that all human beings need three things: (1) the need to belong; (2) the need to have significance; (3) the need for reasonable security. Without these three things the personality is immature and unhealthy.

The first need is the need to belong. Belong to what? Obviously not to yourself, for that would produce a stunted personality. The belonging is a belonging to something outside yourself and something higher than yourself. I listened to two able speakers in differing languages say: "The first need of human personality is personal freedom." I put up my question mark. The first need is not personal freedom but personal bondage: Where shall I bend my knee? To what shall I give my ultimate loyalty and allegiance? Until that is settled nothing is settled. If you "belong" to the wrong thing all life will go wrong with it. Make "personal freedom" your primary concern and it will be the freedom to tie yourself up in knots, to be a problem to your self and others. If your surrender is to anything this side of God it will let you down. No matter how good the thing to which you attach your ultimate loyalty is, if it is this side of God it will let you down. In the Congo at the "Overflowing Heart," Burleigh Law, a devoted and able mis-

79

sionary and pilot, said: "I used to have an experience of God, but I've lost it. My wife became supreme in my life, and because she is such a strong, dominant person, and because I loved her so, I subordinated my life to hers. She became God to me. But now I have become emancipated. I've surrendered to God. And because I love God supremely and my wife subordinately, I love her the more—and safely." Incidentally, when the Communist rebels took over the Wembo Nyama Mission station and held the missionaries hostages, they promised to allow the women and children to be airlifted to safety. Burleigh Law was assigned to take them. If the missionaries were seated at the runway he was to not to come in, but if standing he could. They were seated. But he couldn't bear not to come in as the women and children were waiting, so he came in. He was shot by a rebel soldier. A missionary wife said to me: "He died for us." He was free to live or die—he belonged to Christ.

The sense of not belonging to anything real and eternal is the central insecurity of our time. A man after he died was found to belong to twenty-seven clubs, he added quantity to make up for a lack of quality. He belonged to everything—and nothing, nothing real or eternal.

This sense of not belonging and hence of having no significance and hence no security, makes life inwardly disrupted and outwardly disruptive. The "rogue elephant" in India, Burma, Ceylon becomes "rogue" when he is put out of the herd by the younger males. Since he doesn't "belong" he becomes rogue—tears up trees, gardens, huts, villages, anything in his pathway. Ninety-five percent of delinquencies among young people comes out of broken homes. Having no security in the home, hence none in themselves, they spread insecurity to others around them—they are destructive.

Surrender of the very self to the Highest—to God—is a psychological necessity, a life necessity, as well as a religious and spiritual necessity. A psychologist wrote a pamphlet entitled, "The Therapeutic Value of Self-surrender."

As I sat in a meeting someone quoted Harry Denman: "That which is behind you is greater than that which is before you." I looked at the man seated in front of me. He had a pack of cigarettes protruding from his hip pocket. That was "behind" him. When he was "down" he reached for a cigarette as "a pick-me-up." But what goes up must come down. So he must increasingly reach "behind" to face what is "before." Of all the fragile support in life, that is the most fragile. A man threatened by heart attacks was told by his doctor to give up smoking and golf. He exclaimed: "The two things I want most to do in life—smoking and golfing—I can't do." He didn't "belong," not to anything real, eternal. Had he belonged to Christ he could have taken the loss of both in his stride.

A man said to a friend of mine: "What do I need with God? I have three million dollars in the bank." My friend replied: "You had better read in the Bible the parable of the rich fool." "Isn't that harsh?" he replied. "No harsher than life," said the friend. A long silence followed.

81

What does life say? This: A woman said to me, "I don't have to work. I have money. But I work to keep from committing suicide. My husband doesn't have to work. He has money. He works to run away from himself." Here they had everything—and nothing. They didn't "belong." Hence life had no significance and no security. If you don't surrender to God, you have to surrender to emptiness, to despair, to a life of unhappiness.

In a plush hall in Montevideo, Uruguay, a young woman came up to me after an address: "You are happy with Christ, now tell me how to be happy without Christ." I had to say that I could not tell her how to be happy without Christ. It simply can't be done. Can the lungs be happy without air, the heart without love, the eyes without light, life without life? When you surrender to God you surrender to that for which you are made, you surrender to your destiny, you fulfill yourself. A surgeon speaking in a church said: "If you don't surrender to God, you will have to surrender to me as a surgeon." He might have added, "or to a psychiatrist," "or to your family doctor," or to all three! For you live life against life. Carlyle once said: "Sin is, has been, and ever shall be the parent of misery." And the central sin is the sin of trying to make your self God. It can't be done. So sin is not only wrong, it is stupid. The word "evil" is the word "live" spelled backwords. It is an attempt to live life against itself. The sin of sins is self-centeredness. Self surrender is the central necessity in life.

I asked a woman who had to begin life again after

twenty-nine years of married life: "What was at the basis of your divorce?" She replied: "Liquor and women. He said he wanted his freedom." He got his freedom to have liquor and women, and now he is free, free to face life— with cancer! His freedom has turned to ashes. Had he surrendered to Jesus Christ and not to his appetites and impulses, he would be able to face life even with cancer. For he would have eternal life now.

Alice Means, a devoted missionary in India, faced death by cancer: "I don't belong to death, death belongs to me. I belong to Christ. I was never so happy as I am right now." She had fulfilled the need to belong, she belonged to Christ. She was not a decaying physical being, she was a child of God; being made in the likeness of the Son of God, she had "signficance," untouched by death; she had "reasonable security," for she belonged to "a kingdom that cannot be shaken," not by death or any other happening. When you "belong" to Christ everything belongs to you.

5

Is Self-Surrender Acquiescence?

Does surrender, surrender to God, imply acquiescence or control? At first sight it seems to be acquiescence, you surrender to another. Now do you resign yourself to whatever comes, letting this "another" do everything for you?

At a New Year's retreat held in Washington for many years, government officials and other prominent men and women meet from ten to five to get spiritual resources to face the coming year adequately. One New Year I spoke on "self-surrender." The Secretary for Defense who was present was asked to say something at the close. He remarked: "I liked everything the speaker said except that he kept using the word 'surrender.' I'm afraid I can't use that word for I come from a place, the Pentagon, where that word wouldn't be very popular." I replied, "If you surrender to God, you don't surrender to anything else." He replied. "Then that's all right."

Whether it is acquiescence or control depends upon

the god to whom you surrender. Jesus said: "My Father worketh hitherto, and I work" (John 5:17 KJV). God our Father is a creative God. Science says the same: God, or something, is creating millions of tons of matter every day in an expanding universe. If God is still creating the universe then, at the first creation, it was not a finished creation. God looked upon that first creation and saw it was good. Good but not perfect. It was good for His purposes, the purpose of creating creatures who would become creators along with Him. In that perfecting of the universe they would help perfect themselves. It had to be a universe of resistances—resistances which would make our environment an emery wheel to shape and polish our characters.

The King James Version says: "And we know that all things work together for good to them that love God" (Rom. 8:28). We know that *all things* do not of themselves necessarily work together for good. The Revised Standard Version puts it thus: "In everything God works for good with those who love him." God rescues out of everything some good, if we will cooperate with Him. Note the change: "*with* those who love Him," not "to," but "with." With our cooperation God can rescue out of everything—good, bad, or indifferent—some good. If that is the Christian position, then this is not acquiescence but control.

Paul puts it in these revealing, potent words: "To this end I am toiling strenuously with all the energy and power at work in me" (Col. 1:29 NEB). "I am toiling strenuously"—the human; "with all the energy and

85

power of Christ at work in me"—the divine. The human and the divine work together in "control."

The Christian in surrendering to the Highest in the universe—God—and cooperating with Him and His laws aligns himself with supreme power and love and wisdom and "controls" by surrender and obedience—the highest type of control.

Paul calls this offering of your very selves "a living sacrifice," "your reasonable service." Man arrives at his highest level of rationality when he has sense enough to surrender himself to God. It is the sanest moment of a man's life when he does it. From that moment life begins to add up to sense.

In the midst of writing this comes a letter from a brilliant young engineer in India: "The Ashram at Sat Tal did bring me a new message of hope in self-surrender. Everything becomes very easy after surrender. I have just been wondering if surrender is not the easiest way of getting out of troubles and getting nearer to God. With all the change I got at the Ashram I think it is the foundation for greater things which I am yet to build with all the future in front of me. I think it makes all the difference to live with God and without Him. Your message that out of all calamities and bad things we can mold for ourselves the best is sound and workable. I feel quite convinced that if we work on this 'law' life will never end in failure. This is the key to success which can open to us treasures hidden and unknown otherwise. . . . I am doing fine in my job as head of gear design section. Someday I hope to become a really good gear expert. I quite realize I cannot do it alone, there has to be an energizer—my God." He had discovered the "Law," the law of self-surrender producing a unified person and hence a better gear designer. He has discovered how you can gear into God by self-surrender and gear into nature to become a more competent gear designer. You are meshed into God and nature.

All this fits in with the statement of Jesus: "This is my Father's glory, that you may bear fruit in plenty and so be my disciples" (John 15:8 NEB). The Father's glory is in what? Rainbow thrones, chanting angels and men—is that His glory? No, God's glory is in producing men who bring forth fruit in plenty—His glory is in creating creators. That means God is interested in control, not acquiescence.

This sums up the Christian attitude: "In Him who strengthens me, I am able for anything" (Phil. 4:13 Moffatt). "In Him, not in myself, by surrender to and abiding in Him, I am strengthened as a person, all my powers are heightened, a plus is added to everything. As a result, "I am able of anything." Anything! Healed at the heart, I can say to life: Come on life, come on problems, come on death—"I am able for anything."

So the Christian faith is not a No, but a Yes. This verse sums up its affirmative character: "The divine 'Yes' has at last sounded in him, for he is the 'yes' that affirms all the promises of God" (II Cor. 1:19-20 Moffatt).

Until Jesus came religions were a negation, a No. The Hebrew faith had become a set of prohibitions, the Law, pursued by the Pharisees, the Separatists; a No. The

Stoics in shutting out sorrow had to shut out love and pity—a No. Buddhism, believing that suffering and existence are one, had to cut the root of desire even for life— a No. Vedantic Hinduism, in wanting to get from the personal to the impersonal Brahma is a No to human personality. Brahma is *neti*,—not That, Not that—a No! The world is *maya*, illusion, a No! Modern materialism, in affirming that life is a combustion of chemical elements like a flame which flares up and is then reduced to an ash, is a No! Modern hedonism is summed up in the last words of an actor: "Let down the curtain, the farce is done"—a No! Bertrand Russell said: "Doom falls upon man, pitiless and dark." A No!

At the end of the recital of the No-verdicts on life, "The Divine 'Yes' has at last sounded in him, for He is the 'Yes' that affirms all the promises of God." He does not verbally affirm "Yes" to life as a philosopher, "He is the Yes." The Yes is His very person.

And yet it is no cheap, easy Polyanna Yes. It is a "Yes" with scars on it. It is a Yes won out of a No, an Easter morning won out of a cross. He turned the worst thing that can happen to man, a cross, into the best thing that can happen to man, redemption.

What are some of the promises of God which Jesus affirmed by His Yes? (1) Life is good, but evil has invaded it. (2) Goodness is natural, evil is unnatural. (3) Evil has been conquered—"I have overcome the world." (4) Life can be redeemed, a new birth is possible. (5) Life can be lived, sometimes in spite of everything. (6) Life can be reinforced and can become adequate, the

Holy Spirit is available. (7) Life can be made into a higher form—"changed into his likeness." (8) Life as a whole can be redeemed, the prayer: "Thy kingdom come," will be fulfilled. (9) Death is not an open grave but an open door to eternal life. (10) Life lived on a lower level often says No! Life lived on the level of Jesus always says Yes!

A holy island in Japan is so sacred that neither a birth nor a death may take place on it, both would pollute its sacredness. That sacredness is a No, to birth and to death.

Jesus cleansed both birth and death by a manger and a cross. Jesus said: "Now ye are clean through the word which I have spoken unto you." He cleansed the universe of the many gods and goddesses and gave us the one holy God, our Father. The gods of self-seeking adoration gave way to the God of self-giving sacrifice. He cleansed the family from polygamy to one-man, one-woman loyalty till death parted them. He cleansed prayer from self-seeking benefits to the benefit of self-surrender. He cleansed greatness from having a great many servants to serving a great many. He cleansed life from a basic pessimism to a basic optimism. He cleansed religion from acquiescence and turned it to control.

Jesus is the Great Affirmation. He affirms the most radical proposition ever made to the mind of man, the proposition that the present unworkable world order, based upon greed and self-seeking, be replaced by God's order—the kingdom of God based upon self-giving service and love.

6

Is Self-Surrender Workable?

We have tried to trace the fact that self-surrender is basic in the character of God as seen in the supreme manifestation of God, Jesus of Nazareth, and we have seen it become basic in the best psychological outlook and procedure. But is it workable in this work-a-day world of ours?

What about human relations—don't you have to assert yourself instead of surrender your self to get along with people? If you take the self-surrender attitude will you not be everybody's doormat? Everybody's doormat or everybody's temple of refuge?

Paul gives this principle: "Be subject to one another out of reverence for Christ" (Eph. 5:21 RSV). Notice he does not say, "Surrender yourselves one to another." You surrender to God—and to God alone; you are subject to man. If you surrender to man, it makes man your final allegiance. That final allegiance can only be given to

90

God. But you can, and often have to, be subject to man, reserving the final allegiance to God.

This verse gives the key to how you can be subject to man and still retain your self-respect. The subjection is "out of reverence for Christ." You surrender to Christ and now you can afford to be subject to man out of reverence for Christ. You are subject to man for His sake. That saves your self-respect, for in subjection to someone else you don't do it because you have to, which would mean a master-slave relationship, but because you choose to do it for His sake. That saves the relationship and it saves your self-respect. The alternative is resistance and a refusal to be subject, which means fight, which means that the relationship breaks down. A girl called Mary was attending to her sister-in-law after a severe accident that left her bedridden. After attending to her for months, which involved bedpans, her sense of duty wore thin and she, in carrying out a bedpan, revolted and said: "O Jesus, I'm sick of this." And He replied: "Mary, I want to attend to your sister-in-law, but I haven't anyone to do it for me except you. Couldn't you do this for her, for My sake?" "Oh, yes, I can do it for Your sake. That transforms everything." And it did. The subjection was a sacrament, a joy. Her sense of duty to her sister-in-law became a sense of service to Jesus. Plodding duty took wings.

But there is a relationship in which subjection is really surrender—the relationship between husband and wife. A colleague on an evangelistic tour in China said something to me which I've never forgotten. He said: "There can be no love between husband and wife unless there is mutual self-surrender. Love simply cannot spring up without that self-surrender to each other. If either one withholds the self, love cannot exist." He was profoundly right.

You cannot love Christ unless you surrender to Christ. That is at the basis of many who sigh in our Ashram "Open Heart" sessions: "I want to love Christ and to know Him better." But their lives are still in their own hands, surrendered to nothing except themselves. Then they wonder why they do not love Him or know Him better. You know that which you love, and you love that to which you are surrendered.

If self-surrender is necessary to loving relations to God and in the home, it is just as necessary to right reactions in all our relationships. Why is it that with the best of intentions from the will many react badly to life and their situations? Usually the root of wrong reactions is the unsurrendered self. A pastor and his wife made plans, on their way to one of our Ashrams, to separate; their married life, they thought, was intolerable. But at the Ashram they surrendered themselves to God. When each got rid of the barrier of the unsurrendered self, they came together like two magnets. They reported that they went back from the Ashram "as on a honeymoon." The wrong reactions to each other came out of the unsurrendered self. Now they are happy with each other and effective in their pastoral work.

Many are correct in their actions, but they are wrong in their reactions. The actions are usually determined by the will, but the reactions come out of the subconscious, and the subconscious is where the unsurrendered self lurks. Touch it and it will blow its top. The modes of life come out of the conscious, but the moods of life come out of the subconscious. So the conversion of the actions is important, but the conversion of the reactions is just as important or in some ways more important than the actions. Without a complete self-surrender the conversion of the reactions is impossible. For reactions spring from the subconscious, and the subconscious is the residing place of the driving urges—self, sex, and the herd or social urge. The center of these three is the self-urge, it is the dominant urge. Whichever way the self-urge goes, the other two go with it.

You cannot convert the self-urge by suppressing it or lecturing it or acting as though it weren't there, or dressing it up in the cloak of principles. It can be converted in one way and only in one way—surrender the self to the lordship of Jesus Christ.

This passage makes it clear: "Let us behave with decency as befits the day: no revelling or drunkenness, no debauchery or vice, no quarrels or jealousies! Let Christ Jesus himself be the armour that you wear; give no more thought to satisfying the bodily appetites" (Rom. 13:13-14 NEB). Note that "quarrels and jealousies"—sins of the disposition—are bracketed with "no revelling or drunkenness, no debauchery or vice"—sins of the flesh. And the remedy for both is: "Let Christ Jesus himself be the armour that you wear; give no more thought to satisfying the bodily appetites." The

93

"armour" must be something more than external, it must
be something deep down, so deep that your very thought-
life is changed—"give no more thought to satisfying the
bodily appetites." A fundamental surrender of the self to
Jesus Christ has set up an inner loyalty to Him that ex-
pels the very thought of satisfying the bodily appetites.
It is the expulsive power of a new affection, expelling the
lower by the higher. Since Christ Jesus has possession of
the central self now sex and herd urges come under this
new dominance. Our reactions come out of that central
allegiance, we react in His Spirit and not in the spirit of
the old touchiness and jealousy. Our reactions are christianized.

Jesus said: "Or else, how can one enter into a strong
man's house, and spoil his goods, except he first bind the
strong man? and then he will spoil his house" (Matt.
12:29 KJV). The "strong man" could be the unsurrendered self. You cannot "spoil his goods"—the sex
urges and the herd urges—unless you bind the strong
man, the unsurrendered self. When he is bound by surrender and held by cords of a new allegiance and love,
then the "goods" come under the same loyalty as the
self.

This binding of the strong man and spoiling his goods
can be seen in the case of the disciples before their self-
surrender and receiving of the Holy Spirit. The strong
man kept cropping out. I once swam across a lake, and
when I arrived at the other shore and put my feet down
a lot of bubbles arose from the decaying matter in the
ooze. We can see ten bubbles arising to the surface of

the lives of the disciples from the unsurrendered selves. (1) Selfish egoism—they quarrelled over first places. (2) Self-righteousness—"though all men shall be offended because of Thee, yet will I never be offended," a "they" . . . "I" relationship. (3) Resentments—"Shall we bid fire to come down from heaven and consume them?" (4) Spiritual impotence—"Why could we not cast it out?" (5) Critical attitudes—"Why this waste?" (6) Group bigotry—"We forbade them for they followed not us." (7) Race prejudice—"Send her (a Syro-Phoenician) away, for she crieth after us." (8) Selfish acquisitiveness—"We have left all to follow Thee, what do we get?" (9) A dislike of self-sacrifice—"Be it far from Thee, Lord, this shall never be." (10) Fear—"behind closed doors for fear."

Three years of companionship with Jesus and the knowledge that He had risen from the dead did not bind this strong man—the unsurrendered self. Knowledge is good but not good enough. A complete self-surrender and the coming of the Holy Spirit within them did bind the strong man. They were no longer sitting on a lid holding down the strong man with constant eruptions. The Holy Spirit did bind the strong man in a new, effective way—He took over the three urges and set them to work for the kingdom. He did not suppress them—He dedicated them. The self was now expressing itself in dedicated service; sex, the creative urge, was now creating on another level, creating new movements, new hopes, newborn souls; the herd urge was now fastened on the kingdom of God as the supreme loyalty, and now they were emancipated from the herd so they could serve the herd—"delivering thee from the people to whom I send thee."

Now their urges, no longer at war with themselves, were turned from destruction to construction. The divine Yes at last was sounding! And the world heard it, in fact, it "turned that world upside down."

If you do not take self-surrender as your life strategy, what are the alternatives? Will they work?

This year I heard two verdicts on life: one, "Put out your candles, lightning has struck the world"; the other: "Put out your candles, the sun is up." One verdict leads to a vast pessimism, the other to a vast optimism. Which is true?

Lightning does seem to have struck the world, and all our values seem devastated. The author of "The Third Revolution" says there have been four great humiliations of man: (1) The Copernican—the earth was no longer the center of the universe with the heavens revolving around it; it is a small planet revolving around another center. This is the cosmic insult. (2) The Darwinian— man is nothing but a chance departure from lower animals, the biological insult. (3) The Marxian—man is determined by economic factors in the environment, the cultural insult. (4) The Freudian—man is determined by lower urges in the subconscious sphere, the psychological insult.

Each of these tend to belittle the significance of man. Lightning has struck the world and has reduced man to insignificance, hence the pessimism underlying and permeating this age.

But there is another statement beginning in the same way, but ending in an entirely different outlook and verdict: "Put out the candles, the sun is up." This is taken from a book in which Lin Yutang, the Chinese writer, tells of his return to Christianity after renouncing it and wandering in the barrenness of secularism. He ends one of his chapters with these triumphant words: "Put out the candles" (the dim half-answers), "the Sun is up" (Jesus is alive and available). The half-answers fade in the light of His countenance.

His answer is the answer to pessimism about man. Surrendered to God life takes on meaning, significance, value, goal. How can the person surrendered to Christ look down on the man for whom Christ died? How can man reject what Christ accepts? How can he despise what God loves? The moment you surrender to Christ all your values, struck down by the flash of lightning of modern man's self-sufficiency without God, are restored with a plus. For Jesus Christ is not a lightning flash, blinding you for a moment and followed by the thunder of doom, He is not lightning but light, the full-orbed sun, the sun that never goes down. "He that followeth me shall not walk in darkness." And moreover: "While you have the light, trust to the light, that you may become men of light" (John 12:36 NEB). You not only have light, but as we trust to, surrender to the light, we become men of light. We think light, believe in light, act light, and become men of light. The surrendered

97

Christian is light to any situation in which he finds himself. As long as he thinks Christian, acts Christian, is Christian, he is always light. Every departure from the Christian standpoint is darkness, with no exceptions.

When we ask, "Is self-surrender workable?" the answer is, nothing else is workable. If you don't ally yourself to God by surrender, you ally yourself to pessimism, to hopelessness, to negativism, to futility, to frustration, to cynicism, to self-destruction, to a No!

In the New Testament (Mark 5:1-16) is the account of a man who had his dwelling "in the tombs"—he surrounded himself with symbols of death, for he had death within him. "He would cry aloud among the tombs and on the hill-sides and cut himself with stones," bent on self-destruction. And yet "when he saw Jesus in the distance, he ran and flung himself down before him, shouting loudly, 'What do you want with me, Jesus, son of the Most High God? In God's name do not torment me'" (NEB). He was naturalized in "torment" and any healing invasion of his torment was further torment!

Why? "Jesus asked him, 'What is your name?' 'My name is Legion,' he said, 'there are so many of us.'"

"My name is Legion"—that was the basis of his torment, he was not one person, he was many persons, and many contradictory persons, "a walking civil war." And yet he was religious: "what do you want with me, Jesus, son of the Most High God? In God's name do not torment me." He, like many, had just enough religion to make him miserable, miserable enough to set up a conflict instead of a concord. If you don't surrender to Christ, you surrender to chaos.

A troubled modern man said: "I have too many twos in my life. I have two houses, two cars, two women—I am two persons." "A house divided against itself cannot stand." Inward division is the basis of the modern misery. One man said: "I am a committee"—debating with himself, a self that wanted contradictory things. Another man said, according to a typographical error: "I commute with myself," when he really meant to say: "I commune with myself." Many commute with themselves, meet themselves coming and going in contradictory directions for contradictory ends. In the "Morning of the Open Heart" these statements were heard: "My personality is a double personality, I'm a hypocrite." "I'm a street angel and house devil." "I'm very self-conscious. I like myself very, very much. I'm dressed as a deaconess and therefore people think I am thinking of God, but I'm not."

Whether it is the case of the man dwelling in the tombs, or the man or woman in the office amid respectability, the problem is the same—a divided self. There is no way out of that divided condition except self-surrender to God. That surrender brings one into unity of person and unity of purpose and unity of goal. Note: "When they came to Jesus, and found the man from whom the devils had gone out sitting at his feet clothed and in his right mind, they were afraid" (Luke 8:35). Afraid of what? Sanity! They had become so used to insanity that sanity seemed insane, so they were afraid!

99

This age is so used to the upset, frustrated, unhappy, divided people that it feels afraid of the sanity of self-surrender to God. But self-surrender is the sanest thing a man is ever called on to do. It is sense, yes, Sense!

The shipwreck of Paul and his companions is a picture of modern man: "When day broke they could not recognize the land, but they noticed a bay with a sandy beach, on which they planned, if possible, to run the ship ashore. So they slipped the anchors . . . set the foresail to the wind, and let her drive to the beach. But they found themselves caught between cross-currents and ran the ship aground, so that the bow stuck fast and remained immovable, while the stern was being pounded to pieces by the breakers" (Acts 27:39-41). They found themselves caught between cross-currents—that is the modern dilemma, in both East and West. In India a Hindu said to me: "I don't know to which century I belong. I go into my home and I am in the sixteenth century, and I go outside and I'm in the twentieth century." The man of the West goes into his church and finds currents going one way, the Christian way, and he goes outside and steps into currents going the other way —he is caught between cross-currents. And worse still, he finds those outside currents flowing into and through the churches. The result? If the church doesn't stand for something, its members will fall for anything. The result is confusion.

The predicament of modern man is confusion. Our doctors' offices and mental institutions are filled with people who are passing on their mental, emotional, and spiritual confusions to their bodies. They suffer from cross-currentitis.

Being caught in cross-currents can be disastrous, but the further developments in this particular shipwreck can be more disastrous: "ran the ship aground, so that the bow stuck fast and remained immovable, while the stern was being pounded to pieces by the breakers." If modern man is free to maneuver amid the cross-currents he may make his way through, but if the bow of his ship is caught in fixed formulas, fixed and rigid dogmatisms, then the rest of his life is being pounded to pieces by the breakers.

If Jesus is the center of your faith and surrender to Him is the center of your loyalty, then you have a maneuverable position. Cross-currents may strike you and breakers may pound you, but you do not go to pieces. But if you are stuck in the sands of fixed doctrines and dogmatisms, then you are pounded to pieces by the breakers.

Surrender to Jesus Christ as a person gives you something fixed and unfixed, static and dynamic. He is fixed in history, but He is dynamic and beyond history. When you belong to Him you belong to the unfolding. The more you see in Him, the more you see there is to be seen. You know you have arrived, and yet you are always setting out. It is all an adventure in discovery. A surprise is around every corner. He can never be outgrown and outworn. You belong to the undecayable, the eternally fresh.

To sum up this chapter: Is self-surrender workable?

I would give an unqualified reply: Negatively, nothing else is workable. If you belong to anything less than God it will inevitably let you down without exception.

Positively, self-surrender is the most emancipating, the most universalizing thing imaginable. You don't have to belong to this group or that group; you don't have to be in line with any apostolic succession; you don't have to attain to a certain degree of goodness; you don't have to be educated, rich, or cultured; you don't have to be young, old, this color or that. You have to be willing to give you, the only thing you own—and that alone! You don't have to believe this doctrine or that—*you have to be His.*

Self-surrender is workable, for it works to the degree you work it. Nothing else does.

7

The "How" of Self-Surrender

Everything we have been saying converges on one question: How? After a meeting a lawyer came up to me, grasped my hand as in a vice and said: "Man, how?"

The first preliminary step in self-surrender to God is to be poor enough to receive, to be receptive. It is no mere chance that the first beatitude is this: "How blest are those who know that they are poor; the kingdom of Heaven is theirs" (Matt. 5:3 NEB). There are those who believe the Sermon on the Mount is a new law, a demand laid upon the will, more spiritual and more inward but the same Jewish law, thou shalt do this, thou shalt not do that, a demand and not an offer. The Sermon on the Mount is not practicable, says a theological professor. Of course it is not, not if it is a law.

But this first verse of the Sermon on the Mount cancels all that. It is an offer, an offer to those who are poor enough to receive it: the kingdom of Heaven is theirs.

All the resources of the kingdom are behind you, at your disposal if you know how to take them. This introduces us to grace—not to law. This strikes the note in the opening sentence of the Sermon on the Mount and makes it not a new law but a new offer of grace. Everything in the rest of the Sermon is possible through grace.

This first verse takes you out of a vast whipping up of the will—"I'll try harder"—to a surrender of the will. The verse could be translated: "How blest are those who are surrendered and receptive, for the kingdom of Heaven is theirs." So the first step in self-surrender is to see that it is the open door to God's everything. You don't have to be worthy, to be deserving, you have to be willing, willing to surrender, not this, that, or the other, but the essential you. That "you" takes in all you have and all you expect to have, an all-inclusive you!

The second preliminary step is to remember in the back of your thinking that you are surrendering to a God who not only demands self-surrender, but who has given and still gives and forever will give self-surrender—it is His basic characteristic. At the basis of this act of yours is a basic characteristic in God. You are responding to His initiative of self-giving. You are not doing something that is a marginal act in the universe, you are doing the central thing which this universe holds and demands— self-surrender. It is the very central law and offer at the heart of the universe and God. It gives you confidence that the sum total of reality is behind you as you do this. You are not being queer, you are being natural, supernaturally natural. Rufus Moseley calls it "a happy yielding to God's initiative."

The third preliminary step is that in self-surrender you are fulfilling the very purpose for which Christ died: "His purpose in dying for all was that men, while still in life, should cease to live for themselves, and should live for him who for their sake died and was raised to life" (II Cor. 5:15 NEB). This verse, seldom used as the purpose of His dying, reveals the very heart of that purpose: should cease to live for themselves. The purpose of His dying was to save men from their sins? Yes. From hell? Yes. But primarily it was to save men from self-centeredness, from the sin of making themselves God, the center of all sin, and to release them so they would "cease to live for themselves." When you are surrendering to God you are fulfilling the central purpose of the atonement.

With the fourth preliminary step you can find the clue to your surrender to God in the stages you go through in setting up a close human relationship. In a close human friendship eventuating in a real marriage there are these five actual stages:

1. The stage of drawing near. This is the Yes and No stage. It is the tentative, explorative stage. You want to and you don't want to, you blow hot and cold. The self is afraid to commit itself and yet it wants to commit itself. It is tired of this self-isolation and yet it hesitates to give it up, afraid of change.

2. Then comes the stage of mental decision—the mind is made up. The mind no longer debates, it decides. There may be marginal questions, but the center

has given way, given way to decision. The debate becomes a voice: I'm going to belong to that other person. Mentally you are on the march, a march out of the old into the new.

3. Now we are ready for the stage of passing from the decision to action, to doing it. You actually inwardly let go, you belong to that person. Nothing is weighed out or measured, nothing that the eye can see, but down deep you belong to that person. The tension has turned into trust and the trust has turned to entrustment, you entrust yourself to that other person, to sink or swim, for life or death, to survive or perish. It is done.

4. Then you pass into the stage of inner unity. Having given to that other person the most precious thing you have—yourself—you are now free to take from the other the most precious thing he or she has, the self. A mutual acceptance of selves takes place. You belong, unconditionally. Now love springs up and becomes the atmosphere, the climate, the motivating of the relationship. Love guides the actions, the planning, the directing of two lives together.

That love relationship continues as long as there is self-surrender at the basis of the relationship. But if either one withholds the self, then love refuses to spring up, or if it has sprung up it dims or dies.

5. The stage that ensues is one of continuous mutual adjustment of mind to mind, of will to will, of being to being by continuous mutual self-surrender. The big self-surrender is made when you are married inwardly

and outwardly. That doesn't have to be done over again, in a real marriage it is once and for all.

A couple told me a few days ago that they were celebrating their twenty-fifth wedding anniversary, and that they were going to repeat their marriage vows to each other again. Note, "repeat their marriage vows" as a reminder, but not as a remarriage. That is once and for all in a real marriage. When I asked a group: "Suppose you would go to your wife and say, 'Dear, let us be married over again,' what would she say?" A missionary spoke up and said: "My wife wouldn't say anything. She would go off and weep."

But while there is a once-for-all surrender in marriage, there is a continual surrender, too. For while there is one big Yes in a real marriage, there are a lot of little yeses under the big Yes. Day by day things come up that need to be adjusted, to be surrendered, to be conformed to the big adjustment. So there is a once-for-all surrender, and there is a continuous, day-by-day surrender. There is a growth in surrender. Self-surrender is a continuing principle as well as a once-for-all practice. It is a way of life, a very important way of life. Self-surrender in daily things is a catharsis. To be able to say day by day: "I am sorry, I was wrong" is a cleansing attitude of mind.

We have now before us the various stages we go through in setting up a warm, workable human relationship in friendship or marriage. Will it be different in setting up our relationship with Christ? I say with Christ instead of with God, for many have trouble with God. In Sweden a teacher, after making a very careful analysis

107

of herself, said: "I'm afraid of God. I can't surrender to Him." I replied, "Suppose you think of God in terms of Christ. Suppose God is a Christlike God, could you love Him?" She thought she could. She surrendered to this Christlike God and was a new radiant person.

So now we take these consecutive stages in our surrender to Jesus Christ. *First you draw near—the explorative, tentative stage.* It is a big thing to turn over the one thing you own, your very self, to another. You want to and you don't want to. You are afraid it is a leap in the dark, and if you leap it may land you in an abyss of doubt and fear. So you hesitate. Don't be afraid of this upset condition. God has to upset you on one level to set you up on a higher level. This is a constructive upset.

Then you come to the *second stage—the stage of decision to belong to Him.* You weigh the alternatives: I can belong to myself alone, or I can belong to Him. If I belong to myself alone I make myself God. But I'm not God—God is God. I am ready to belong to Him. That is my destiny. I'll fulfill that destiny. I want to belong to Him. I will.

You are now ready for the *third stage: Since I have made up my mind to belong to Him, I will implement it by putting my will behind the mental choice.* I actually do belong to Him from this moment. And I will act as if I belonged to Him. Since the mind and the will are in agreement about it, the emotions will sooner or later give their approval. But even without the approval of the emotions you belong. So begin acting "as if." And

108

thank Him by faith. First faith, then fact, and then feeling.

The *fourth stage* is the outcome of the last one: *Having given your very self to Him you are now bold to take His self—your all for His all.* Being love He will take you as you are. He will not require conditions, standing you up in the corner until you are worthy to be received. He will take you as you are and begin to make you what you ought to be. You are now one. All He has is yours. Through identification with him you now begin to learn to take from Him. You are now strong in His strength, pure in His purity, loving in His love, victorious in His victory, "In the world you shall have tribulation, but be of good cheer, I have overcome the world." Not will overcome, but *have* overcome. So you overcome in His overcoming. You live no longer on the unit principle, but on the co-operative plan. You supply willingness and He supplies the power. "Round our incompleteness flows His completeness, round our restlessness His rest." You are now living by grace. That sense of orphanhood is gone, you are now accepted and belong, belong not to this or that marginal thing or person, you belong to the very center, you belong to *Him.* Now nothing else matters. This is it!

But while everything seems to be settled and you have arrived, nevertheless this is just a beginning, for this is the way and not the goal. You now enter the *fifth stage, the stage of continuous mutual adjustment, the stage of growth.* You have said "All" to Him and He has said "All" to you. But there are a lot of little "alls" under the big "All." They will come up day by day and little surrenders will have to be made, made about things and issues you did not realize would be involved. So the surrender is a blanket once-for-all surrender, but also an unfolding surrender. As you have given all you know and all you don't know, the "don't knows" have to be dealt with as they arise. How? By a continual surrender. You do not fight or suppress the issue, you turn it over to Him and say: "I am Yours and this thing concerns me, so this is Yours, too. I surrender it. Tell me what to do about it." That keeps problems and issues from piling up and making you tense and burdened. It is a continual catharsis. You are saved from the tension that comes from suppressing things and driving them into the subconscious sphere where they fester, and also from evading the issues in which case they nag us from the margin of consciousness. You are fulfilling that verse, "But if we walk in the light, as he is in the light, we have fellowship with one another, and the blood of Jesus his Son cleanses us from all sin" (I John 1:7 RSV). By walking in the light, holding nothing back, you have a continuous fellowship with Christ and a continuous cleansing of your problems and sins. It is a working way to live.

This daily and hourly continual surrender saves you from the psychiatrist's couch where you have to unburden yourself through torturous months and years of piled-up problems, resentments, fears, self-preoccupation, and guilts buried in the subconscious.

It also takes the place of the confessional where weekly you unburden yourself and gain a doubtful absolution by penances. In the case of the psychiatrist and the priest it is secondhand—this is firsthand. You are in unbroken contact with your Redeemer.

You are also emancipated from tranquilizers and sleeping pills, for you are tranquil through surrender and hence sleep without drugs. You are free—in Him!

Before we leave the How? we must face a snag that sometimes holds us back. First, "I am willing to surrender some things but I'm not willing to surrender my self." Use this prayer, if it really expresses your condition: "Lord, I'm willing to be made willing." Then surrender your hesitation.

Second, "I am willing now, but will I be able to live this?" At the moment, with your present resources and your past experiences, it seems impossible. But with a complete self-surrender you are not now with the old resources based on a self-centered and self-reliant you— you are now a new you, with new resources, new direction, a new attitude, a new faith, not in you but in Him, you are a new everything. Act as if that "new everything" were now beginning. He who began a good work in you will complete it. You don't have to live a lifetime now. Live day by day, moment by moment. The future will take care of itself. And that future is as bright as the promises of God.

8

"One Remedy"?

In the Introduction I mentioned a woman who came up to me at the close of a meeting and said: "I've found you out, you have only one remedy—self-surrender!" In this chapter I pick up the Introduction and discuss whether self-surrender is the "One Remedy."

Late last night I had a telephone call from a distracted woman. She and her husband had been in my meeting. Her husband had asked their eighteen-year-old son to go to the meeting. The son said he had his studies to do and besides he didn't want to go. The father commanded him to go, the son was stubborn and angry. When the parents returned from the meeting the father was furious with the son for not going and ordered him out of the house. While the mother was telephoning me the son was standing on the street corner and the father was in the house, both angry and unbending. What was the problem there? The unsurrendered self on both sides.

Nothing would untangle that situation unless one or both would say, "I'm sorry." In other words, surrender.

In an airport in India our plane was tied up. A pilot had spoken roughly to one of the airport attendents. The ground crew, in sympathy with the attendant, refused to service the plane. So the passengers, their engagements and connections in jeopardy, sat helpless while represen-- tatives haggled. One thing and one thing alone could untangle that snarl: "I'm sorry." That happened and the traffic began to flow.

A newspaper strike went on for a year and a half in India. A subordinate was rude to a superior officer. He was dismissed. The other employees went out on strike until he be reinstated. A Christian government labor official suggested: "Let the dismissed man who was rude acknowledge his wrong and ask forgiveness. Let the officer forgive him and reinstate him." This was done and the strike was over. Headlines: "A novel way to settle a strike." "A novel way?" No, it was sense, it was the only way out of that impasse, self-surrender on both sides!

In our relationship with God, with ourselves, and with one another the key to every logjam is self-surrender. And where does self-cultivation come in? It comes in after surrender. You cannot cultivate an unsurrendered self. It is on the wrong center. You cannot discipline or cultivate a self which is off-center. The center must be changed to Christ by surrender. Now centered in Christ you can discipline and cultivate this new self in a new center. Now infinite growth is possible. With nothing between you and this redemptive Christ you are being exposed daily, hourly, momently to His redemptive stimulus. This exposure is physical, mental, spiritual. Your whole being is exposed to the divine Yes. A plus is added to all you think and say and are. You are cooperating with creative Love, you become creative.

That exposure to this cooperative Love is found through the Quiet Time, preferably in the morning, in the pure strong hours of the morning when the soul of the day is at its best; through sharing with others what you have found; through daily and hourly obedience.

This self-surrender to Christ is the sovereign cure for loneliness. How can you be lonely when you are not alone? People ask me, where do you live? And I have to tell them: "Wherever my suitcase is." For fifty years my home has been in my suitcase. I can sympathize with the man who stuck a label on the inside of the lid of his suitcase: "God bless our home." But I know nothing of loneliness. I cannot remember when I've had a blue hour or a discouraged one for forty years. He has been here, there, everywhere. Therefore never a dull, lonely moment.

But without personal self-surrender there is no cure for basic loneliness. Television, books, concerts, crowds, entertainments may distract you momentarily, but when you get away from them the basic loneliness sets in again. With basic contact with Him you have a sense of at-home-ness anywhere in the world. You are never a stranger and no land is a strange land, you are at Home. He is our Home.

Self-surrender not only takes away loneliness, it takes

away fear of death. It takes away fear of death because you have already died, you have died to you as the center of you. Your self has been crucified with Christ: "I am crucified with Christ." Only those who have already died are not afraid of death. As someone has said: "As far as the self-surrendered are concerned, the undertaker has come and gone." But now that I am crucified with Christ —it is not the ordinary crucifixion, there is a resurrection in His crucifixion and there is now a resurrection in your crucifixion—"nevertheless I live"—and how! I am alive to my fingertips. "Yet not I, but Christ liveth in me: and the life which I now live in the flesh I live by the faith of the Son of God, who loved me and gave himself for me" (Gal. 2:20 KJV). That sentence from Paul is gloriously mixed—you can't tell where you end and Christ begins and where Christ ends and you begin. Death is swallowed up in victory. You cry: "If this is death then blessed be death—it is Life." A radiant soul in dying said to me: "They tell me this is death—it is Life!" She welcomed death: "O Death, throw open the gates." If you belong to Christ death belongs to you. George Mac-Leod says that "the only man who cannot be broken is one who is already broken"—broken by his own consent.

Another side product of self-surrender is the possibility and aid it gives to surrendering burdens that arise daily. When the self is still on your hands the daily burdens, produced by the unsurrendered self, cling around that unsurrendered self and make the burdens doubly burdensome. But once the self is surrendered a lot of

115

burdens automatically drop off because they had been produced by the unsurrendered self.

Many burdens come from our environment, whether the self is surrendered or not surrendered. The principle and practice of self-surrender helps in the practice of burden-surrender. After the supreme surrender of the self it is comparatively easy to surrender the burdens as they arise. My key verse in regard to burdens is this one: "And the government shall be upon his shoulders" —His shoulders, not mine. Since He is the owner, He can now be the governor and take the daily burdens of government. Not that I can wash my hands and let Him do all the deciding and executing—that would produce irresponsibility in me—but when I surrender the burden to Him I ask Him: "Now show me what you want me to do about it." That makes it a joint responsibility. The burden is on Him, I am relaxed and responsive and cooperative.

A woman came to our Ashram and in the "Open Heart" session, where we tell our needs, she said: "I've come here to find out how to manage my family." Note she used "manage." Deep down she wanted to boss her family. When she surrendered her bossy self to Christ a great burden was lifted, she no longer had the thorny job of managing her family, all she had to do was to love them, and the management took care of itself in large measure. For "there is nothing love cannot face" (I Cor. 13:7 NEB).

A young man came to our Ashram and in the "Overflowing Heart" said: "I've resigned as the general manager of the universe." The surrender of the self had cut him down to size and had cut his job down to size—something that God and he could manage together.

I asked an Indian Christian layman working in the income tax office: "What's your biggest headache?" thinking he would have lots of headaches in his job. He was surprised at the question and replied: "I'm a Christian, I don't have any headaches." The government was upon His shoulders.

On the other hand, a burdened man said to me: "I'm a two-ulcer man in a four-ulcer job." The government was not upon His shoulders. As I write this in a plane headed toward Atlanta, Georgia, I'm reminded of what a medical officer there said to me: "Seventy-five percent of the heads of departments in the great corporation I serve have stomach ulcers. I don't know what to do for them. I was trained to treat people physically for physical ailments, but these men are suffering from physical ailments that are rooted in the spiritual. I don't know how to deal with that." Both doctor and patients needed to surrender themselves to God.

A farmer's wife, herself radiant through self-surrender, took hold of the coat lapels of a big industrialist in his home and said: "Bill B., what you need to do is to surrender to Jesus Christ." He scarcely realized what was happening to him, but soon he was on his knees surrendering himself. He arose different, transformed. He dictated a letter to the farmer's wife and to me, telling what had happened to him, turned to his secretary at the close of the dictation and said: "Now you know me."

117

She quietly and thoughtfully said: "Mr. B., you have what we all need." He called the whole factory together and told them what had happened and said to his men: "If you get down and discouraged, go to the prayer room, on company time, and surrender yourselves and your worries and tensions." Summing up what had happened to him, he said: "I had been giving my money to God all my life, but I had never given myself." When he finished teaching his Sunday school class of young adults, a young woman said to him, "Mr. B., you did not get that out of a book." No, the big industrialist got it on his knees in self-surrender.

So self-surrender, once-for-all, with daily self- and problem-surrender, along with continued obedience in big and small, is the answer.

A businessman, without preliminaries, began an interview with me: "I'm trying to live the Christian life but I'm having a hard time of it." When I asked him what he thought was the matter, he replied: "Well, twenty times a day this self of mine will say to me, 'I'll give up here and I'll give up there, but please let me stay at the center.'" I replied: "You've got your finger on the problem straight off—self-surrender." When we rose from our knees his tensions were gone, for Christ instead of self was at the center of his life.

Several years later I met him again. "Do you know me?" he ask. I have difficulty with truth at that point, so I replied: "I do and I don't." He reminded me about our last meeting. I exclaimed: "You're not that man." "Yes, I am." "But you're different." "Of course I'm different." And he was—very, very different. His wife came up and said: "Thank you for giving my husband back to me." My reply: "I didn't give him back to you. He gave himself to Christ and Christ gave him back to himself, to you and to all of life." His hard time had turned to a heaven of a time. Hell turned to heaven on the turnstile of self-surrender. The moment he belonged to Christ life belonged to him. His life sums began to add up to sense, total sense and meaning.

If this can happen among the laity, it can and does happen among the clergy. For many clergymen give up everything to be a clergyman, everything except the clergyman. Jesus said: "If any man would come after me let him hate father and mother, brothers and sisters, yea and his own self also." Why did He put that last, "yea and his own self also"? Because it is the last thing we ever give up. Yet until we let the self go we are trifling with this business of being a Christian. The Christian life simply cannot be lived unless we surrender the self. A pastor walked home with his wife after preaching what he considered a great sermon. He turned to her and said: "Dear, how many great men are there in the world?" His wife quietly replied: "Dear, one less than you think."

This intrusion of self into church life comes out in many ways, some of them very obvious. Two sisters wanted to build a church but couldn't agree—one wanted a spire on the church and the other wanted a tower. Neither one would give an inch. So the committee decided to put up a spire at one end and a tower at the other, monuments to the unsurrendered selves. A woman

119

promised to give a stained-glass window in a new church on one condition, it was to be a picture of herself. Someone looking at the saints in stained-glass windows defined a saint as "one who lets the light through." But when the light came through this stained-glass window, it revealed not a saint but a self—the self-seeking self. Many inscriptions under gifts read: "To the glory of God and in memory of. . . ." The glory was not to God alone.

There was to be a renovation of a church on account of an educational unit. It involved the moving of the piano to another location. The pianist objected: "I've played this piano at that place for twenty years and I'll not play it at any other place." The pastor quietly replied: "Your resignation is accepted." She lived with a sulky resentful self the balance of her days. "Behold your house is left unto you," said Jesus to a nation. The word "desolate" is left off in later versions. "You want your house—I give it to you," He said in essence. The empty house, empty of all but self, was the pay-off, the punishment. "Father, *give me*" was the first step down for the prodigal son, the far country with its hunger and misery was the end produce. "What will you *give me*?" was the first step down for Judas. Suicide of the self he couldn't live with was the end product.

Many, although not coming to a tragic and dramatic end, spend their lives with a troublesome unsurrendered self, spoiling their own happiness and the happiness around them, until something jolts them into the necessity of self-surrender.

Sometimes we look for evidence of surrender, resulting

120

joy, instead of centering the surrender in an act of the will, leaving the emotions to take care of themselves. As I have said, the order is: first faith, then fact, then feeling. You give yourself by faith and believe that He accepts your gift, feeling or no feeling. You begin "to act as if"—the faith turns to fact and the fact to feeling.

We do not say that self-surrender solves all our problems. That depends on the follow-through and the carrying out of its implications. But what it does do is to set up right relationships between you and God, you and yourself, and between you and others. It gives you a framework and an attitude in which your problems can be worked out. It puts your feet on the way—the way in general and the way to solve all your problems in particular. For you have the central problem solved—the self is no longer at the center trying to be God, it is in its place surrendered and subordinate and aligned to the Highest.

If you don't surrender to God don't think you don't surrender. Everybody surrenders—to something. Some surrender to themselves as God. If you surrender to yourself as God you won't like your God. You will do as you like and then you won't like what you do. You will express yourself and you won't like the self you express. You won't like your self and no one else will like you. "It's a million chances to one that the self-centered are unpopular," said a psychiatrist.

If you don't surrender to your self as God, you will probably surrender to someone else as God. And if you do you will probably be disillusioned. Every human idol

121

has feet of clay. When the people of Tyre and Sidon heard Herod harangue them, they cried, "It is the voice of God and not man." "Instantly . . . he was eaten with worms and died"—a worm-eaten god. Every person to whom you surrender as God will turn out to be a worm-eaten god.

The French "Mother," the successor to Arabindo Ghose, was heard to say to someone over the phone: "Surrender to me." She, too, was a worm-eaten god—worm-eaten with pretence and hocus-pocus about being God.

If you surrender to the herd, to society, if you do what everybody does and make Society your God, then you will be disillusioned. Someone has said: "If the church is wedded to the spirit of the day it will be a widow tomorrow." For the spirit of the day is a fickle, changeable, undependable ghost. The leading woman of a prominent denominational group in a large state came from the upper crust of a certain town. When she left, the group broke down, three members committed suicide, three went to a mental hospital, all the couples but two were divorced, and one couple is shaky. Centered on the herd they fell apart personally and collectively. Fasten your loyalty and love on anything this side of God and it will let you down. But when you surrender to God without reservation, everything within you cries out: "This is It."

A doctor tells of his being called to see a patient, the head of a large corporation, who was having increasing attacks of asthma. During the last attack it looked as though the patient was not going to pull through. But

122

the doctor could find no physical basis for the asthma, so he asked him: "Is something troubling you?" The patient replied: "No, doctor, I'm a member of the church. I'm an official in the church, nothing is troubling me." The doctor went away puzzled.

The next day the patient sent for the doctor. The patient said to him: "Doctor, I told you last night that nothing was troubling me, but I've been talking to God all night. I looked at the ceiling and saw in bright letters the words: 'Seek first the kingdom of God.' On the walls the same words: 'Seek first the kingdom of God.' On the floor the same words. Now, Doctor, I've not been seeking first the kingdom God. I've been seeking first the kingdom of John Brown. I've climbed to the top of this corporation, but I've done it ruthlessly, caring nothing of what happened to others. I've been a completely self-centered man. But something has happened to me: I'm seeking first the kingdom of God." The doctor said: "I went away with the tears streaming down my cheeks. I had seen the birth of a soul."

This doctor saw the birth of a soul through self-surrender. But self-surrender means not only the new birth of a soul, it means the birth of everything—new relationship to God, to yourself, to society; new outlook on life, new method of dealing with daily problems, new power to face whatever comes, new sense of inner unity and of belonging, new resources to live by—new everything.

9

Victory Through Surrender!

Everybody surrenders—surrenders to something, some-one, or Someone. The alternative is not whether to sur-render or not to surrender. We all surrender, from the moment two cells, the sperm and the ovum, surrender to each other to form a new life down to the moment where our bodies are surrendered to the grave. I repeat, we all surrender. Some of these surrenders are built in necessities to surrender. We have to surrender if we are to survive. The babe must surrender to the necessity of the mother's breast, to the necessities of sleep and elimination, to co-operation with its surroundings. These are built-in neces-sary surrenders. But some surrenders are optional, option-al with results or consequences. We are free to choose, but not free to choose the results or consequences of our choices. They are in hands not our own. Some go through life choosing to surrender to the right person and to submit to the right things—they get results; the sum total of reality is behind them, they have cosmic backing for their way of life. But some go through life surrendering to the wrong person or persons and submitting to the wrong person or things—they get consequences; they are up against reality, they are frustrated, in trouble with themselves and others.

A doctor and his wife faced this choice. To what should they surrender? She was bitter and resentful and full of fears, for her husband had an affair with another woman. He was defiant, asserting his right to be free to do as he liked. They were both Roman Catholics, but the wife's need drove her across denominational boundaries to seek for help. In one of our Ashrams we pointed her to Christ and not to Protestantism. She found Him through self-surrender. All her bitterness, her resentments, and her fears dropped away. She was on top of her impossible world. She had victory—victory by surrender. And it was a victory *in spite of*. She decided to stay within the Roman Catholic fold. We accepted her decision—gladly, for we had fellowship in Christ, not in folds.

What kind of victory was the husband having? A friend went to see him and found him walking the floor with a whisky bottle in one hand and tranquilizers in the other. Here was a man of high intelligence, a medical man, surrendering to his own supposed freedom and finding himself a slave to stimulants and sedatives—stimulants to buck him up and sedatives to tone him down. He was free to tie himself in knots. His wife was free to have

125

peace, to develop, to have victory—in spite of. One surrendered to his own impulses and found himself a victim; the other surrendered to Christ and found herself a victor.

An army officer, attending the New Year's retreat for government officials and other leading men and women in Washington, said to his mother: "Mother, I have come to the conclusion that we army officers are fooling ourselves when we think that we are having a good time in our drinking parties. You Christian people are the really happy people, the rest of us are in a make-believe happiness—it's unreal. Yours is real," He bought some of my books, had them wrapped up and took them home with him. Driving along in his car another car pulled up alongside his and the driver called out to him that a parcel of books had fallen from his car. He had picked up the parcel and put it on the curb a block or two back. The man turned back and found the parcel on the curb. He felt a strange Providence, like the Hound of Heaven, following him. It was so. He read one of the books, surrendered himself to Christ, was soundly converted, and is now partaking of that joy which he sensed from afar, but didn't realize until he surrendered. He found victory through surrender.

A woman in an office was the contagious center of ill-will. Her ugliness of temper and spirit permeated the office. One day the boss, who had recently come into a new life through surrender, greeted her, not with the usual "Good Morning," but with the words: "Have you heard the good news?" And when the woman asked,

"What?" he replied: "That God loves you." The woman sat down at her desk without a word. Soon she went off alone and surrendered her bitterness of attitude and word and, deeper, her bitter self. She was transformed. Now she is, as the boss puts it, "the spark plug of love and goodwill, and as a consequence the atmosphere of the whole office is different." Victory through surrender!

A man and his wife were at cross-purposes. Each was standing on his or her own rights. She felt she had a right to stay in bed in the mornings and let her husband get his own breakfast. So she stood on that right, or rather, she lay on it. She came to one of our Ashrams and made her surrender to Christ and was converted. When she asked: "What shall I do when I get home?" she was told that she should go and tell her husband that she was the cause of all their troubles. "Oh," she replied, "I couldn't do that! That is the point at issue. I say he is the cause and he says I am." "Well," we said, "you go and pray about it." She went home and got up the next morning and prepared her husband's breakfast, which intrigued him. But he couldn't help his usual dig: "Well, Miss High and Mighty, what did you learn at the Ashram?" She replied: "I learned that I've been the cause of all our troubles." She got up from her chair, came around beside him and knelt, folded her hands and said: "Please forgive me. I'm the cause of all our troubles." Telling about it afterwards she said: "He came near upsetting the table to get down on his knees beside me. He blurted out, 'You're not the cause of all our troubles—I am.'" There they met each other—and God. Each surrendered to

God, then they surrendered to each other and were free! Now that couple, instead of pecking at each other, is one. They are now a team going out and witnessing to others as to what surrender to Christ can mean, and they are winning many to the Way. They both found victory through surrender.

Whether it is a once-for-all surrender in a life crisis or a day-by-day surrender of the problems of life as they come up, the way out is—victory through surrender.